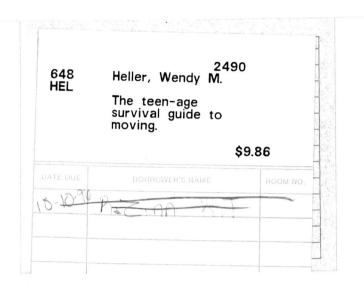

648
HEL

2490

Heller, Wendy M.

The teen-age
survival guide to
moving.

$9.86

DATE DUE	BORROWER'S NAME	ROOM NO.
10-10-90		

2490

648
HEL

Heller, Wendy M.

The teen-age
survival guide to
moving.

ALTERNATE LEARNING CENTER
LUCAS COUNTY OFFICE EDUCATION

The Teenager's Survival Guide to Moving

T * H * E
Teenager's Survival Guide to Moving

by Patricia Cooney Nida, Ph.D.
and Wendy M. Heller

ATHENEUM New York

Library of Congress Cataloging in Publication Data

Nida, Patricia Cooney
The teenagers survival guide to moving.

Includes index.
SUMMARY:
Explains how to survive and grow, emotionally and practically, during the stressful life changes
related to moving, how to keep old friends and make new
ones, how to adapt to a new school and community,
and how to cope with an overseas move.
1. Moving, Household—Juvenile literature.
[1. Moving, Household] I. Heller, Wendy M.
II. Title.
TX307.H45   1985   648'.9   84-21543
ISBN 0-689-31077-3

Atheneum
Macmillan Publishing Company
866 Third Avenue, New York, NY 10022
Collier Macmillan Canada, Inc.

Designed by Mary Ahern

3 5 7 9 11 13 15 17 19 F/C 20 18 16 14 12 10 8 6 4 2

Composition by Dix Type, Inc., Syracuse, New York
Printed and bound by Fairfield Graphics, Fairfield, Pennsylvania

To Ross Nida

Contents

Acknowledgements

We would like to thank those whose ideas, insights, and support contributed to this book: Dorothy Heller, Shirley Rosenkranz and her students, Carmen Rey, Sidney and Karan Morrison, Bill and Christine Garlington, and United States Air Force Chaplain Ralph Neilsen; as well as Thomas Holmes, M.D., and Richard Rahe, M.D., for their work on life change and stress, which is drawn on in Chapter 2; Robert Seidenberg, M.D., for the concept of loss of credentials; and Albert Ellis, Ph.D., whose work on rational-emotive therapy is the basis of "straight thinking." Grateful acknowledgement is made to Kendall/Hunt Publishing Company, Dubuque, Iowa, for permission to use material from Moving Your Family, *by Patricia Cooney Nida, Ph.D.*

Introduction

Let's Get Moving!

Most of us have faced the prospect of moving at least once. For some, it's a way of life. Every year, one in five American families changes its residence. Some families relocate many times; it's not unusual for a military family to move seventeen times during a twenty-year career in the service.

Families move for many reasons. You may be moving because your father or mother has been transferred, or because your parents are looking for better job opportunities in another city. You may be moving because of a divorce or a death in the family, or because one family member has to live in a particular climate for reasons of health. You may be moving to a smaller house or to an apartment because, in these difficult times, your family needs to cut down on its expenses.

Moving means more than just changing your address. It means changing many major aspects of your life—your school, your teachers, your activities, your friends. And change is always difficult, even if the change is for the better. You'll have exciting new experiences and make new friends; but no matter where you're moving, you can expect some things to be different. Adjusting to new things always takes work.

Even if you're only moving to another part of town, your house and your neighborhood will be new. The farther away you go, the more things will be different. If you're moving to another geographical region, you may find yourself in a new environment and an unfamiliar climate. Different regions of the country also have different types of housing, schools, and even customs. If you're moving overseas, you'll be expecting such differences, but they also exist within the United States. People in one town may routinely drop in on a neighbor; people in another may not even know who lives next door.

No matter where you go, you'll meet some pleasant surprises and some unexpected disappointments. When Jessica's father, a sales representative, was transferred from Massachusetts to Southern California, it meant a promotion and a raise. Jessica hoped they might be able to have a pool and maybe even a tennis court. But her family was horrified to learn how expensive housing in their new town was. Even with Dad's raise, they could only afford a house half the size of their wonderful old home in New England. And the nearest tennis court was at the public park. After they moved in, they were even more upset to find that not only was their new house expensive, but it seemed flimsy and poorly constructed too. Only later did they come to understand that it was not a case of shoddy construction, but regional custom. By February, Jessica's family was beginning to appreciate their new hometown on its own terms. While New England was under a blizzard, Jessica was playing tennis at the park in shorts. Because of the mild weather, the houses in their new town simply didn't need the heavy construction and insulation of homes in the East.

Whether this is your first move or your tenth, whether you're moving across the street, across the country, or overseas, pulling up roots can be painful. Although it's hard on everyone in the family, it can be especially hard on teenagers. When adults move, they concentrate on the physical work of moving—packing the boxes, cleaning out the basement, and figuring out what to do with that hideous painting cousin Ralph gave Mom last Christmas. But when teenagers move, they concentrate on the feelings that come with moving—the anguish of leaving friends, the anxiety of fitting into a new school, the loneliness of not having anyone to talk to at lunch.

This book will not tell you how to pack your

physical possessions for your move, but it will tell you how you can understand and handle the emotional side of moving with your family. Families, of course, come in all forms. You may live with one parent or both; you may be an only child or have brothers and sisters. You may not even live with your parents at all but with relatives or other adults. As you read this book, try to see how each suggestion fits your own situation. If it talks about parents but you live with your grandmother, the concept can still apply to you.

There are many things in your life that you simply can't control. But there are other things you can control. You may not be able to do anything about your family's decision to move, but you can control many aspects of your own personal move by how you think about it, feel about it, and plan for it. By taking responsibility for your own move, understanding what you and your family are going through, and being prepared for the feelings you are going to experience, you can make your transition to your new town a success.

1

Your Moving Experience

The Phases & Emotions of Moving

A SENSE OF LOSS

Any time you make an important transition from one part of your life to the next—such as graduating from school, getting married, or even moving—it is a time for strong emotions. When you move, it becomes very clear that you are ending a chapter in your life: you're actually going away! In order to go on to the new, you must leave behind the old, including people who are important to you—friends, teachers, and sometimes family. You need not lose these relationships forever when you move, but the fact remains that you are going away while they are staying behind, so you're likely to feel a sense of loss.

Even if you're happy about the move, sooner or later you will feel some grief for the part of your life that is drawing to a close.

Alex was excited when he learned that his father, an army master sergeant, was being transferred to Hawaii. He was glad to be leaving the small town in North Dakota where his family had lived for three years. He didn't think he'd ever miss *that* place with its bitter winters. Everyone in Alex's family was always complaining about the cold and the isolation. And who wouldn't want to live in Hawaii! But a few months after Alex moved, he was surprised to find that he was homesick for North Dakota. He missed his friends on the hockey team, and he even missed his grumpy old coach who had taught him to be a goalie. Alex had gotten pretty good at ice hockey and cross-country skiing, and there certainly wasn't any of that in Hawaii.

The years Alex had lived in North Dakota represented an important chapter in his life. The friendships he had made there were strong ones and meant a lot to him. The landscape of North Dakota might not have been as glamorous as tropical Hawaii with its fern forests and orchids, but it was home to Alex. Only after he left did he realize just how much he had grown to love it. Although Alex felt his move would be an improvement, he still experienced a sense of loss in an unexpected way.

WHAT WILL IT BE LIKE?

When you move, you must also face the unknown, and this always causes some anxiety. Even if you have visited your new town and are excited about living there, you won't really know what it will be like. You may know there's a good drama program at your new school, but will you make the soccer team? And, most important of all, will you make new friends as good as the ones you're leaving behind?

If your family is moving because of a parent's job transfer, there's a good chance you won't know anything about your new town or even the part of the country where you will be living. Does it really never rain in California? Does everyone wear cowboy hats in Dallas? What will it really be like to live in Saugatuck, Connecticut?

It's natural to feel that the prospect of moving to a new place is a little scary or depressing. You've got a good "mental map" of your old town; you know where everything is and how to get where you need to go. But when you move to your new town, you won't know your way around at first. How do you get to school? To the library? To a hot fudge sundae? Eventually you'll build up a mental map of your new town, but it will take some time before you feel as comfortable there as you did in your old hometown.

A PREDICTABLE PATTERN OF UPS AND DOWNS

Although each family's move is different, the problems they must face, the anxieties they suffer, and the decisions they have to make are much the same. The moving process itself triggers certain—often strong —emotional reactions in people as they go through the move from beginning to end. Based on what psychologists have learned about the ways people react as they undergo change, you can expect to experience a series of emotions as you go through your move. These emotions tend to occur in a predictable pattern, and if you know what to expect, you won't be caught by surprise.

Although you will feel some negative emotions during the change process, you will also feel excitement, anticipation, and happiness as you look forward to the good things ahead of you—adventure, travel, new experiences and friends. This combination of negative and positive feelings can be very confusing. At times you may feel as if you're on a roller coaster of emotions—up one moment and down the next. But remember, there's nothing wrong with you: these strong and contradictory feelings are a *normal* part of the moving experience.

What can you do about it? Psychologists say that just recognizing that a problem exists and talking about it can help a lot. Understanding why you are feeling the way you are, thinking about the change, and talking about it with others can help you overcome its effects.

NATURAL REACTIONS TO CHANGE

Isolation. When people experience change and the anxiety it brings, they naturally want to retreat from it. They may unconsciously try to escape from the change, thinking that if they ignore it, maybe it will go away. But when they retreat from it, they also isolate themselves from others around them.

Mai's mother had been talking about nothing but their upcoming move to Washington, D.C., ever since she was hired as managing editor of a famous magazine. She was excited about her new job and preoccupied with the details of the move. Mai didn't even want to think about *that* subject. Her mother tried to involve her in conversation, but Mai only wanted to be alone. In her room, listening to records, she could "escape" from the move. She felt she was losing a part of herself and that her mother simply wouldn't understand. Mai's mother was hurt. She wanted Mai to be happy about this important step up in her career. She didn't understand the hurt her daughter was feeling.

Misunderstanding. When people isolate themselves from each other, they stop communicating. They stop talking to one another and they stop hearing what others are saying. If that happens, you may feel

terribly alone and unable to talk to anyone about
what you're feeling. When all the members of a family feel this way, there is likely to be misunderstanding, which may easily lead to anger and arguments.

Resistance. Another natural reaction to change is to
resist it. You may feel you just can't live through the
move. It's too emotionally draining, and there's just
too much hard work to it: packing the boxes, sorting
old clothes to give away, and before Thursday someone's got to get the cat vaccinated! You may find
yourself wishing you could just go back to the way it
was before the move.

Poor Planning. The disruption that comes with moving often makes people plan poorly. Moving becomes
the full-time job of the whole family. And still nothing seems to go smoothly. No matter what day the
movers are coming, there's no way your family can be
ready. They need three more weeks!

It's not your family's fault. Most people just
aren't very good at moving. The normal routine of
life has been upset for everyone, and they're suddenly called on to do a lot of extra tasks. Suddenly,
life is no longer focused on normal things like going
to school, being with friends, and toilet-papering the
varsity quarterback's front yard the night before the
big game. Now, all of life seems focused on The
Move. Instead of asking you, "Have you done your
homework?" your mother may be nagging you,
"Have you gone through your closet yet?"

People often underestimate how much work it is

to move. They don't realize just how many extra chores they have to do, and they don't leave themselves enough time to do them. Even if they are experienced at moving, they sometimes forget from one move to the next. Because there are so many different things that all have to be done by Moving Day, you and your family will need to plan more carefully than usual and budget time for the unforeseen things that always come up at the last minute.

THE PHASES OF THE MOVING PROCESS

You may have thought that moving was only what happened on moving day. But it's not so simple as that. Your move doesn't take place when the moving van drives up, or even when you walk into your new home and unpack. It's a process that you must evolve through gradually. It begins when you first hear about the move and doesn't end until you are completely established in your new home—many *months* later.

You know that if you want to move a stereo or television set from one place to another, you have to unplug it first. If your equipment is complex, the process may be even more complicated than that. You may also have to disconnect cables or antennas or speakers—all the things your set needs in order to work. Only after you have disconnected everything can you safely move the object to another place and plug it in again.

In a way, people are like that too. The moving process has three phases: the *Disconnect Phase*, when you unplug yourself from the old place, the *Change Phase*, when you make the physical move, and the *Reconnect Phase*, when you plug yourself into your new environment. Those are the stages that people *should* go through, if they want to have the best possible move with the least amount of trouble. When people don't go through the whole process, they have problems. Imagine what would happen if you tried to move your stereo or TV without disconnecting it first. You could damage the cord or ruin the equipment if it's a complicated set with lots of attachments. And if you don't reconnect all the parts again after you move it, it just won't work the way it's supposed to.

You are even more complex than your stereo or TV, so you need to be "handled with care" when you move, too.

THE DISCONNECT PHASE

Kent's family was just finishing dessert one evening in Colorado Springs when his father announced that the company he worked for had transferred him to the corporate headquarters in New Jersey. The family would have to move in two months, he said. Kent took another bite of his strawberry shortcake. I ought to be feeling something, he thought. But I don't feel anything at all!

Shock is usually the first reaction to news of a coming change. If you find you don't feel anything at all when you first hear of the move, don't let it fool you. You're probably just numb. It seems as though this *thing* isn't really happening to you, and you may try to deny it. "Dad's company won't do this to us," you tell yourself. Because you just can't believe it, you may avoid talking about the move or preparing for it. When Kent learned he would be moving to New Jersey, he didn't think it would really happen. So he didn't talk about it. In fact, he didn't even tell his friends he was moving. Were they angry when they found out from someone else! They thought Kent didn't care enough about them to tell them the important news. But in fact Kent couldn't believe it himself.

If you feel nothing when you first learn of the move, you may falsely think you'll get through it without any problems. Shock is the mind's way of cushioning itself against a blow. But after a while, the shock wears off and it begins to dawn on you just what you're losing because of the move.

Anger. When Norm first learned he would be moving from Chicago to Philadelphia, it was okay with him. He was a Revolutionary War buff and looked forward to exploring the historical sites he had read about. But within a few weeks he realized that his father was planning the move for the day track season opened. Norm had been working hard for two years to make the varsity team. Now he wouldn't even get a chance to try out for it! He was furious at his father for making him move.

As the reality of the move hits you, you're likely to feel angry. Although you're really angry at the move, you may find yourself directing your anger toward those who are closest to you—your parents, your brother and sister, your friends, or even your German shepherd. Or you may get angry at yourself. In Maureen's family, when tensions erupted into quarrels, Maureen thought it was her fault. It seemed to her that every time she was around her parents, there was an emotional explosion. If I wasn't here, she thought, they wouldn't have so many fights.

During the moving process, everyone in the family is likely to be more on edge than usual. Parents may snap at each other or at their kids for no obvious reason. The anger and frustration they feel because of the move may explode in your direction even though you don't deserve it. A month before Leif's family was to move, he walked into the kitchen just as his mother was hanging up the telephone. She had just learned exactly how much it was going to cost to have their grand piano shipped from Asheville, North Carolina, to Seattle, Washington. When Leif came in wearing his Walkman, she exploded at him for listening to "that music," and added, "if only you'd kept up your piano lessons, it would somehow make it more worthwhile."

Leif was stunned by her anger. He had only walked into the room—he hadn't even tracked in dirt or banged the door. His mother's anger seemed completely irrational, but Leif could see that, for some reason, he was getting its full force. He couldn't even guess what he'd done to bring it on. He didn't know that his mother was really angry at the move.

When people are angry but don't communicate, it's easy to misinterpret their actions and think that you caused the problem, even if you don't know how.

Depression. After anger, depression typically sets in. As you await the move, doubts fill your mind. I just can't get through this, you think. My life is out of control. I'll never make new friends. I'll never be on a soccer team again. You feel you couldn't be more depressed than you are—and you haven't even moved yet! Maybe, you tell yourself, it will get better as soon as you get it over with and move!

Panic. During the Disconnect Phase, the hard work and strain of packing and saying good-bye leads to wide swings of emotion. As the moment approaches when there's no turning back, panic often sets in.

No one is more likely to feel panic than your parents, and that can be frightening. We ordinarily think of adults as not being afraid. After all, they're not supposed to be afraid; they're supposed to be in control of the situation. But, in fact, what they are facing is as new for them as it is for you. They don't know what's ahead. And as they seal up the last carton and look around the empty room that was once their comfortable den, they ask themselves, "Did we make the right decision?" Their last-minute insecurity and indecision can be contagious, and you're likely to feel some panic too.

THE CHANGE PHASE

Finally the last suitcase is packed. You've taken the guinea pigs your mother said you had to give away— because she wouldn't have them in the car on the trip —to your friend's house and said good-bye to them. The movers are on the way. From now until you unpack in your new home, you are in the Change Phase. This is the physical move. It may last only a few hours, if you have to drive across town to your new home or fly to another city. Or it may last weeks, if your family has planned a cross-country trek from the old town to the new one.

Just before and just after the physical move, turmoil and tension are likely to be at their peak, but the actual move itself—especially if it is done in a short period of time—may be relatively calm. In fact, your trip may even be fun if you get to see some of the sights and visit attractions along your way.

THE RECONNECT PHASE

After you've moved in, you enter the Reconnect Phase. You begin to plug yourself in again, to reattach all the wires and cables and antennas that you need to have connected before you can get your life back on track and running smoothly. But don't expect things to be back to normal as soon as you unpack your suitcase. It takes time to get settled again. For one thing, you'll probably still be exhausted from the hard work and the move itself. In the new place, you may be overwhelmed at first by new things. But as you begin to get used to your new home, neighborhood, and school, you'll find that a sense of control and of belonging gradually returns to your life.

It's likely you'll still experience some anger and depression after you move in. It's normal to miss the people you've left behind, the familiar sights of your old hometown, the activities you've been used to. After you've lived in your new town long enough, its sights will become as familiar to you as those of your old town, you'll be caught up in activities again, and you'll meet people who become important to you.

DIFFERENT REACTIONS

You may be puzzled when the other members of your family don't seem to share the emotions you're feeling. A month after Norm moved to Philadelphia, he still wasn't used to living there. He still felt like the "new kid" and hadn't met anyone he really liked yet. He missed his friends in Chicago and wished he were back there with them. As he sat in the house wondering if they had already forgotten him, his sister danced through the room laughing and singing to herself. If she's going through the same thing as I am, he wondered, why is she so happy while I'm so down?

As you go through the range of emotions that come with the change process, you may feel happy one day and angry another; one day you'll be sad, and the next—you're just numb. When families go through change together, each individual experiences different emotions at different times. Your sister may be happy while you're depressed, but tomorrow she may be down while you're feeling pretty good.

BLAME THE MOVE, NOT THE PEOPLE

You can't eliminate the emotional ups and downs, but you can reduce their effect by understanding what is happening to you and your family. Remind yourself that the emotions you're experiencing are caused by the move—not by some defect in your personality or by some other person. This will help to defuse the power of the feelings themselves. When you don't know the cause of emotional anxiety, that anxiety becomes even greater because an element of fear is added. You may wonder: What if the problem is even greater than I think? What if there's something terribly wrong with *me*? Is it always going to be like this? Once you can identify the problem, it won't seem nearly so large and menacing. And you'll know where to place the blame: on the move, not on the people.

As you face your move, you may feel as if you're at the entrance to a maze. You used to know the way from point A to point B, but now you don't know which direction to go to get anywhere at all. Remember that you're not alone in the maze. There are others who are trying to find their way through it too. Don't isolate yourself. You'll still have to face the same obstacles and frustrations, but they will be easier to overcome if you face them together.

2

People + Change = Stress

Because people are different, they react differently to the experience of moving. One person may seem to thrive on it, while another may find it very difficult and painful. Yet these same people may have different reactions to moving at different times in their lives. One move may seem easy but the next one surprisingly hard.

Brenda's foreign service family had lived all over the world and felt that moving was second nature to them. By the time Brenda was sixteen, she'd lived in seven different countries. Her family had moved to Brasilia and Berlin and Riyadh without much difficulty, and now they were enjoying their post in Paris, where her father had just been given his most important job yet. Brenda's mother was just finishing her master's degree in French at the Sorbonne when she found out that she was going to have a baby. The family was excited about it, but then came the news that they were to be transferred immediately to London. While they weren't happy about leaving Paris, they didn't think the move itself would be difficult since they were old hands at moving. But soon an atmosphere of tension started to develop in the family until Brenda could hardly stand to come home. And a week before they were to leave, Brenda's mom still hadn't made any arrangements for the movers to come! Her dad seemed to get upset at the slightest thing, and her parents' arguments grew so heated that Brenda started to worry they might want to get a divorce. Why, Brenda wondered, was her family becoming so disrupted over another move, when they'd done nothing but move all their lives?

CHANGE CAUSES STRESS

Moving is something that happens to real people, living real lives that were already busy enough before the order to move came along. Any move takes a lot of work and energy, but if your family already has a lot of other demands on them, the move may be even harder. One critical factor that determines how well you and your family will adjust to this move is how many other things are going on in your lives, right now, competing with the move for your attention and energy.

Whenever something new or out of the ordinary happens to you—you get a new teacher, someone rear-ends your car in the parking lot, you get chosen editor of the yearbook—a change is introduced into your life. These life changes may affect you in many different ways. One particular change may disrupt your daily routine. Another may place new responsibilities on you. Another kind of change may mean you'll have to make some new decisions or learn a new skill. Whatever impact the change may have on your life, it means you now have to devote attention and effort to adjusting to the change. Life is full of such changes, some tiny, some bigger, some gigantic. When you move, you must make so many changes in your life that psychologists consider the moving experience a *major life change* likely to produce a lot of *stress.*

HOW FULL IS YOUR ENERGY TANK?

Handling change requires attention and energy. But no one has an unlimited amount of energy. Think of it like the gas tank of a car. You fill up your tank with gas, you burn up the gas as you drive around, and then you have to fill up your tank again.

You only have a certain amount of energy in your own "energy tank." You use it up as you need it, going through everyday life. But when you're experiencing an unexpected change, like driving uphill, the extra strain on the engine burns up more gas than normal. We say the engine is "under stress" because it's having to work harder to get up the hill. When you have to deal with change, you are functioning under stress too. Like your car, you can only go as far as you have enough fuel to take you. When you use up all your energy, you can find you're emotionally "out of gas" too.

If you're in good health and haven't had many changes in your life lately, your energy tank should be full. You should be able to fly right through a few extra adjustments without much trouble. For you, moving should be fairly simple.

But if you've had to accommodate some other significant changes in your life recently, your energy tank may be running low. The idea of making yet another change may leave you feeling exhausted or fearful. For you, moving may be more difficult and demanding. Take a moment to think: how full is your own energy tank right now?

CHANGE AND YOUR EMOTIONS

Change itself isn't bad or something we should try to avoid. In fact, it's an inevitable and essential part of life. Too much change can be stressful, but not enough change can be unhealthy too. Think of it this way: if your life is going along exactly the same, day after day, you may feel a sense of *boredom*.

Add something new, and your *interest* perks up.

With another change or two, you feel *excitement*.

You look forward to each day's challenges because you've got plenty of energy left to handle them.

Eventually, you reach the point where you feel that your life is perfectly in *balance*. The number of changes in your life is matched by the energy you are using to handle them. You're busy, but just busy enough.

At this point, however, just one more change is one change too many. You feel *confusion*. After that another change brings *anger*.

Pile on still more changes, and you start to experience *fear*. It's just too much and too fast. You're losing control, and your energy is running out.

At a time like this, add just one more change and things seem really hopeless! You just can't cope any longer. You've reached the point of *exhaustion*. You're really "out of gas."

MAKE A LIST

As you prepare for your move, it will help you to look at how many changes you and your family are already handling. This will give you an idea of whose "energy tank" is full and whose is running low. What counts as a life change? Anything new or different in your life or your daily routine; in your relationships with people at home, at school, or in community life. Did you just get your driver's license? Or a part in the school play? Make—or quit—the swim team? Do you have a new girlfriend or boyfriend? Did your old blind cocker spaniel have to be put to sleep? Perhaps your mother has just changed jobs, or been elected to the school board, or just finished graduate school. Did your sister just join Brownies? Did your father's responsibilities increase at work? Make a list of the changes you have experienced in the last year or so. Here are some examples to include, if they apply to you.

* Starting or finishing school
* Beginning a new sport or hobby, or stopping an old one
* Difficulty in school
* Getting a new teacher or coach
* Getting a new responsibility at school (getting elected to the student council, getting a part in the school play, being chosen cheerleader, etc.)
* Member of family leaving home (for school, marriage, or work)
* Getting a new boyfriend or girlfriend, or breaking up with an old one
* Buying, selling, or remodeling your home
* Illness, accident, or death of a family member or close friend
* Divorce, marital separation, or reconciliation in the family
* Separation of the family geographically, for example, because of work
* Marriage in the family
* New baby in the family
* Getting fired or laid off at work

  * Change in the family's financial status (whether good or bad)
  * Beginning a new job
  * Change at work (in responsibility, procedures, work hours, office conditions, boss, secretary, colleagues, etc.)
  * Career change
  * Winning an award for personal achievement
  * Change in religious activities
  * Extended visit by relatives or friends
  * Good friends move away
  * Legal troubles or violations of the law

What other changes can you think of to add to your list?

Count up the items on your list. Pay particular attention to very serious items, such as the death of a family member, serious accident, or divorce in the family. These kinds of changes have a much greater impact on individuals than other, less serious kinds of events.

After making your list, you may be surprised to realize just how many things have really been happening to you and your family. Your move will bring even more change into your life, and make more demands on your energy reserves.

Now ask yourself again how full your energy tank is. After counting up the changes going on in your life, you may feel that your first estimate needs to be revised.

It's important to remember that any life change

uses up your energy, even when it's a good change. When your brother gets married, everyone will be happy about it, but there's going to be a lot of work planning the wedding, the reception, and all the other details, not to mention the sadness that comes with realizing that he won't be living in his old room upstairs anymore.

Just as a new diesel Volkswagen gets forty-five miles to the gallon while an old Cadillac might only get six, the members of your family will differ in the mileage each gets out of their individual energy tanks. Some will be able to handle more change than others before they start to run out of gas. One member of your family may seem to enjoy change while another may quickly feel confused and overwhelmed. However, when people seem to be adapting well to many changes, they may already be at their limit. The coming move could be the one change too many that uses up the last drops of gas in their tank.

SIGNS OF STRESS

When your car is running low on gas, it sputters and coughs before it actually runs out. When your own energy tank starts running low, it gives you some signals before it runs out on you altogether. If you learn to recognize the signs of stress in yourself and in others, you'll know when you need to take action to lessen the tension and fill up your energy tank again.

Most people are aware that outbursts of anger or spells of depression are signs of tension and stress. They also know that stress can show itself in physical symptoms such as high blood pressure and ulcers. But these are not the only ways stress affects people. There are other important warning signs to watch for.

Physical Signs of Stress. Stress can affect health in many ways. The hard work and strain of a move can lead to fatigue, which can make you susceptible to ailments such as colds and flu. Muscle spasm or tenseness can bring on various aches and pains. Is anyone in your family experiencing any of these:

* General run-down feeling
* Colds or flu
* Aches in muscles or joints
* Headaches or toothaches
* Weight gain or loss
* Trouble sleeping or waking up
* Outbreak of hives or allergies
* Increase in craving for food or loss of appetite
* Increased use of alcohol, cigarettes, or coffee
* Drug use

Sometimes people falsely think that stress-caused problems are not real sicknesses but only imaginary. As you go through your move, if you or someone in your family does get ill, it doesn't mean the illness isn't a real one. When stressful changes use up your energy, they also drain away some of the natural resistance you use to fight off germs.

Emotional Signs of Stress. Stress can also affect your emotional well-being. Everyone has bad days now and then, but under stress people may show any of a variety of emotional reactions. Are any family members:

* Irritable or impatient?
* Withdrawn or sullen?
* Forgetful? Having difficulty concentrating, remembering details, or planning ahead?
* Experiencing extreme and rapid mood swings —very happy then very low?
* Quick to anger or "mad at the world"?
* Very depressed or always sad?
* Losing their sense of humor?
* Denying any feeling about the move?
* Losing interest in activities with friends and family?

Early Warning Signs. Change causes stress, but stress also causes change. When the members of a family are under stress, their relationships and communication patterns become altered. Sometimes it takes a long time for the stress to build up so much that people realize that there is a problem somewhere. Before that happens, their behavior toward others in the family starts to change.

Even if no one person may be showing obvious signs of stress, you may notice some changes in the way the family gets along together. Some early warning signs of family tension are:

* Family members insist that everything is "just fine, thank you, fine!"
* Anger seems contagious—it passes from one family member to another
* People drop their responsibilities and make up excuses for irresponsible behavior
* It seems like there's a constant atmosphere of tension in the family
* Communication breaks down completely and family members refuse to discuss or deal with the move

LESSENING STRESS

If you recognize any of the signs listed above, it probably means that the many physical and emotional demands of the move are draining your family's energy tanks. Unfortunately, replenishing your energy supply is not as easy as driving into a gas station and saying "fill 'er up." No attendant can do it for you. It's strictly self-service: you have to do it yourself.

Take Good Care of Yourself. Some teens handle tension by binging on junk foods or by not eating at all. It may seem like simple common sense (and it is), but good nutritious food, adequate rest, and exercise are essential for keeping your energy tank topped off. You may find yourself saying, "Yes, I know that, but I just don't have time today!" You wouldn't wait until your car ran out of gas before you filled it up, so don't wait until you're completely "out of gas" before you start doing something to fill up your own energy tank. Moving time is no time to start a crash diet!

Talk About It. Don't let communication among the members of your family stop. Take plenty of time to talk to one another and to listen too. As you talk together, try to get at the things that are bothering you and making you feel pressured. Then, see if there's anything you can do to eliminate some of those things that are causing stress. Is Mom feeling overwhelmed because the burden of packing is all on her? Perhaps everyone else could agree to spend the weekend helping in a marathon packing session. It just might take the pressure off her enough to ease that feeling of being overwhelmed by all the work.

Sometimes what you need most of all is a talk with a good friend. You need to remind yourself that you still matter to your friends and that they will always be a part of your life. Going to the movies or the Friday night football game with your friends and keeping up your usual activities as much as you can is a good way to keep some of the normal patterns in

your life and remind yourself the world doesn't re-
volve around this move.

If you don't have anyone you can talk to, find
someone, even if you have to go out and search. Don't
forget the people who are always there to help and to
listen when you just need a sympathetic ear—a counselor, priest, minister, or rabbi. At school you'll find a
lot of people you can turn to: teachers and other staff
members, the school nurse, and even the district psychologist. There may be other resources in your community you can call on, such as a youth assistance
organization that holds regular rap sessions. If you
live on a military base, you can seek out a chaplain or
a counselor at the local drug and alcohol or family
life program.

Take Time to Laugh. Don't lose your sense of humor.
Things are serious enough as it is! Let yourself laugh
at the funny things that happen. The mover may
pack the cat-litter box, or you may run across Dad's
old yearbook with a picture of him dressed as a cheerleader—wig, hairy legs and all. Laughter is a good
way to let off steam harmlessly.

Because of the difficult emotional and physical
demands on people when they move, your family will
need to plan for some family fun time—being together without tension. Try going out for a picnic at
the park, or spending an afternoon miniature golf-
ing, or going to a movie. A trip downtown to pick up
cartons at the moving company doesn't count! Do
something that has nothing to do with the move. You

simply have to get away from it once in a while. And it will help your family remember to think of one another not just as packers, sorters, house-painters, and vacuum-pushers, but as people who have fun together and love each other.

3

You're All in This Together

Moving With Your Family

A popular belief holds that happy families and well-adjusted people shouldn't feel any stress when they move. It's an unfortunate misconception, because when people who believe that do experience the normal stress that comes with moving, they start to question their own worth. When Deanne's family moved from Lincoln to Fremont, Nebraska, they thought they would be able to fly right through this move without a problem. It wasn't a long distance; "We're all healthy well-adjusted people in our family," they said. "There's no stress here!" But when Deanne's brother got in a fight the first week at his new school and was suspended, they were deeply shaken. They wondered if something was terribly wrong with them, after all.

No matter how happy the members of your family are, they're likely to experience some stress when you move, because it's a normal reaction to change. Stress has little to do with how well-adjusted you are, but a lot to do with how many other things are going on in your life, and how full your energy tank is when the move comes along. What a family really needs to get through a move is understanding, support, and communication.

THE FAMILY WEB

The family relationship as a group is never more important than at this time, when all of you are going through a demanding experience together. All of you are individuals, living your own lives, but as family members you have a great influence and impact on one another.

The family relationship is rather like a spider's web. The spider spins its web so that each tiny thread is directly or indirectly connected to all the others. No matter where a juicy bug lands on it, the spider can feel the vibration even if he's at the opposite end of the web. When one part of the web is shaken, the rest of it shakes too. And the spider's web is very sticky. Once you get in, you can't get out.

Families are like that too. The members of your family are tied together by bonds like the threads of a spider's web, although those bonds may be almost as invisible. When one member of the family is angry or depressed, it affects everyone else. The shock waves of that person's behavior ripple out through the family, and everyone else can feel them. Feelings are contagious. It's hard to keep your own spirits up when someone close to you is moping around or snapping at others all the time.

Stan's sister Judy was a junior in high school and had just made cheerleader when the family was transferred to Ames, Iowa. She took the move badly and began to pick fights with Stan. This annoyed their mother, and she yelled at their father to do something about it. He felt sorry that his job transfer was causing the family so much pain, but found himself yelling back at them anyway. Every night the dinner table became a war zone. Judy's anger was enough to set the whole family "web" shaking.

You'll also find that your friendship group acts just like a family. It has its own web of relationships, which shakes when one part of it is disturbed. When one member of the gang is under stress, everyone gets upset.

The members of your family will share some worries in common about the move. But, in addition, each one will have individual concerns about very different things. If you know what those concerns are, you will be able to be more understanding toward them and help your family get through the move.

PARENTS' CONCERNS

What are the adults in your family feeling? Whether you live with both parents or in a single-parent household, you'll want to understand the concerns the adults around you are likely to experience when confronted with a move.

We expect adults to be in control of their lives, but the move may be making them feel tension they don't understand and can't control. Yet it may not be obvious what they're going through because they may feel they're not supposed to show their anger or sadness around you. For years, parents have been told that, no matter how terrible they feel, if they put on a cheerful face, their kids will not have difficulty with the move. That's an unfair burden to ask parents to bear. It's almost impossible to conceal our feelings from the people who know us best. Even if your parents do succeed in hiding their emotions, you will still feel the tension in the air. Don't think you caused it or that they're angry at you.

The adults in your family may be having a hard time deciding just how they feel about this move. But rather than share their worries with you, they may stop talking when you walk into the room. It's not that they're trying to exclude you—they're trying to protect you from the anguish and pain they feel.

Under the surface, there may be other, hidden

fears. Is your father being transferred? You might expect him to be happy about the move. But, in fact, he may be very worried about his new job. He will be leaving a workplace he is used to, where he knows the ropes, knows the territory, and knows that the boss goes crazy if anyone throws away a paper clip. His job in the new town is an unknown quantity: it may involve an entirely new position, new rank or new responsibilities for him; it's certain to involve a new supervisor, new coworkers, new surroundings.

Even if the transfer brings a promotion, it may also bring unexpected and uncomfortable changes. Your mom may have been Vice-President in charge of Operations at the East Flyspeck plant, but she may find herself just another mid-level executive when she's transferred to the company's world headquarters in New York City.

No matter what the job level, the transferee is going to have to prove himself—or herself—all over again to the people at the new job. What will the new boss be like? Will coworkers respect the new person's abilities? Most of all, will he or she make a go of it? Today it can cost a company as much as fifty thousand dollars to move a transferee's family, and that represents quite an investment! The transferee is under pressure to prove that he or she was worth the expense.

There may be other pressures besides financial ones. The job itself may be at stake. Randy Greenspan couldn't understand what was happening to his father after he announced their move to Houston. At first Randy's father had been excited and had told Randy proudly that the move included an important position, a promotion, and a raise. But soon afterward, he became tense and often exploded with anger at some little thing Randy or his brother did. Randy was bewildered. He sensed but could not explain his father's fear of the move. What Mr. Greenspan didn't tell him was that the boss had called him in to say, "The Houston project is behind schedule. We're sending you in to get it off the ground by the deadline. If you succeed, it'll mean a feather in your cap, but if you blow it, it'll mean the end of your career with this organization." Naturally he was worried sick about his transfer.

SPOUSES' CONCERNS

When both parents have careers of their own, the move almost always means that one person must give up his or her job. In the past that always meant the wife, but nowadays it can often mean the husband. Today, over half of all women work, and most families depend on that second income just to get by. If your father is being transferred and your mother also works, she'll be worrying about moving *her* job too. Looking for a new job in the new town won't be a pleasant prospect. Having to give up her income, even temporarily, as well as the personal satisfactions of the job, may be difficult to bear.

Randy thought his mother would be happy to

move to Houston, because her parents lived there. But she wasn't as pleased as he expected. When her husband's transfer came through, she had just landed an important promotion she'd worked hard for. The move would mean throwing away her hard-won position and her whole job too, for her company had no office in Houston. The idea of starting all over as a job hunter in a new town, when she'd enjoyed the security of an important job for years, was terribly frustrating to her.

Even if the other parent doesn't work, he or she may still have the frustrating and humiliating experience of starting out all over again as a nobody. Psychologist Robert Seidenberg calls this losing one's "credentials." No one in the new town knows about all the things the person has achieved in the old town. No one in the new community knows that your mother is the world's best church bazaar organizer, or that she won first place for her double-fudge cheesecake at the Gourmet Cooking School contest.

In addition, the nonworking parent usually bears the major responsibility for the physical work of the move. Not only does that mean packing up all the things in your house and finding a moving company, but it includes a lot of other things too: closing out the account at the bank, making sure your little brother's records at the orthodontist get transferred, and what are we going to do about that barrel of crystal stemware that Aunt Lillian left with us for safekeeping before leaving on her cruise to Patagonia?

If your family owns its own home, your parents will be concerned about the details of selling it. Just keeping everything picked up in case prospective buyers drop in can be an unexpected burden. Your family may feel they have vacuumed the living room more times during the months your house is for sale than in all the years you lived there!

Then your family will have to find a new home. House-hunting in an unfamiliar city can be difficult and frustrating. It may involve one or more frantic trips to the new town. Your parents will be anxious to find a nice house or apartment, and they may not have much time to do so. They may not even know where to look for one in a strange town. Will the new place be available by the time your old house sells or the old lease is up? Will the movers arrive with your furniture on time? Will the electric company get the lights turned on when they promised? Moving a family from one home to another is a great feat of organization and planning.

Even if the adults in your family are delighted about the move, they will still have to leave behind much that is dear to them: friends at work and in the community, that favorite beach where your family always went picnicking on the Fourth of July. No matter how good they may feel about the move, they won't feel good about leaving friends and favorite places.

The single-parent family has special concerns. Not only does the single parent have all those worries about the new job, but also the entire burden of moving and house-hunting in the new town. It's true that with fewer people in the house, there are fewer decisions to cause crises, but there are also fewer people to help. With all the extra responsibilities your parent must bear, he or she is likely to be overprotective toward you at this time, so you'll have to be especially understanding. When you were a child, you expected your mother or your father to take care of you. But now, as you near adulthood, you and your parent can actually take care of each other. How can a kid take care of a parent? By being there when your parent needs you—by offering emotional support, understanding, and a sympathetic ear; and even by pitching in to help with a few extra chores or having dinner ready as a surprise when your parent comes home.

BROTHERS' & SISTERS' CONCERNS

Are there other kids in your family? Depending on their ages, your brothers and sisters will have worries of their own about the move. If you understand what their concerns are likely to be, you'll be able to help them through the move and won't get impatient at what seems like silly behavior to you.

It used to be said that children don't react to a move. But today experts recognize that even young children can sense the disruption around them when the family moves, although they don't understand what is really going on.

Babies. In general, children from eight to twelve months of age are afraid of strangers. When you move, everything is strange, so it makes them very upset. They don't like the waitress in the restaurant or the maid in the motel; they only like Mom, your sister, and the dog. And they don't want to sleep in that strange motel room; they want to sleep in their own familiar bed! They need to be reassured by being around familiar faces. Don't try to get them to enjoy all the new things around them. They won't!

Toddlers' main fear is that they're going to be deserted. They need to be assured that the family is going through this together and that they're included in the move. Since small children see themselves as the center of the universe, when they see everyone else in the family upset, they think it is because of them—that no one loves them anymore and that their family is going to move away and leave them. One of the ways they show their fear is by clinging to you. It may be annoying when they want to sit on your lap all the time, but they need that close contact in order to be reassured.

Two-year-olds don't like to move because they don't like anything! They've just learned how to say no, and they spend all their time practicing it. They don't like Chicago, they don't like Grandmother, they don't like going to bed, and they don't want to move, period! Don't let their *no!* upset you. They're not being belligerent just to annoy you. They can't help it: it's a normal stage of childhood. Don't ask them questions that they can answer with their favorite negative word. Give them alternatives they have to choose between: "Would you rather eat the banana or the orange?"

Four- and five-year-olds often act as if they understand more than they really do. In the confusion of the move, if their family doesn't take lots of time to explain things to them, they may develop some curious misunderstandings. When the Lees were getting into the car to go to the airport, five-year-old Heather began to cry and scream uncontrollably, "I don't want to die! I don't want to die!" Her puzzled family couldn't imagine what was scaring her, but after some coaxing, at last she sobbed out the real reason for her fear. Earlier that year, when Uncle Fred had died, Heather had been told that he had gone to heaven, up in the sky. Now the family was going to go on an airplane—*up in the sky,* and Heather was afraid it meant they were going to heaven too.

Often, because no one has thought to tell them, these children don't understand that they are going along on the move. Matthew was very interested in all the preparations his family was making for their move. He knew that Mom and Dad and Jennie and Tommy were going, but he became alarmed when he learned that Tigger the cat was being given away. Using his childish logic, he saw that all the big members of the family were going on the move, while the cat—a small member of the family—was being given away. That must mean, he reasoned, that all the small members of the family were to be given away—including himself! At this age children need to have everything explained to them over and over, until it's boringly clear, and they need to be assured patiently that they're going along too.

Grade-school children are often afraid for their own safety in the new place. They need to know they'll be safe when going to school and won't fall into that big drainage ditch they saw as the car sped by on the way to the new house. They worry that they'll get lost, that they'll have to cross a busy street, that mean kids will pick on them. They need assurance too, but also practical help so they can learn their way around. They are very susceptible to teasing at this time, since they don't really know what's ahead of them. You'll need to be careful how you talk to them. What may seem to you like a harmless remark about mean kids down the block can become a great fear to them.

Grade-school children also experience the grief of having to give up their first real friends and the frustration of starting out in the new town as the new kid. They have to prove themselves all over again, with friends, in school, in sports.

Animals. And don't forget Max the dog. Animals can also react to the turmoil of a move. They know their family well, and they can feel it when people are under stress, even though they can't possibly understand why. From fear, they may run away on moving day, or get sick. They need lots of love, too.

TEENAGERS' CONCERNS

Teenagers' greatest concerns are leaving old friends, making new friends, and being accepted at school. School itself is more important now than ever. Being out of step with the rest of the class is frustrating and harder to overcome than it was in elementary school. Teens also find they must prove themselves all over again in the new school and with new friends.

The combination of a teenager and a middle-aged parent can spark some serious family clashes. Adults going through the period of life known as middle age often find themselves questioning their direction in life; they feel they have a short time left and wonder if they're doing the right thing. Meanwhile, teenagers are at a time when nothing their parents do seems right! When parents start to wonder: Was it right to take the transfer? Is this move the right decision? The teenager in the family may add to their frustration by chiming in a resounding "NO!"

As teenagers move toward the independence of adulthood, they become directed outward, away from the family, and toward their friends. Part of becoming an independent adult is having independent thoughts and feelings, but this often leads to disagreements with parents. Since it is the parents who are responsible for making the family move, the move can become a focus for resentment against them.

Without thinking about it, parents may also find themselves using the move as a way of asserting control over their kids. Sometimes it's hard to let go and realize that their child is an independent person now, and they may unconsciously want to hold onto the old relationship of dependence as long as they can.

HELPING THEM THROUGH IT

You can avoid some of the tensions that occur around the time of a move by understanding what the members of your family may be going through. If you try to look at things from their point of view, their behavior will make more sense to you, and you won't think they're just acting crazy! If you see that members of your family seem sad, upset, or withdrawn, try to find out what's really bothering them. Perhaps there's something you can do to take off some of the pressure, even if it's just doing the dishes when it isn't even your night, or mowing the lawn, or cleaning up your room without being asked to. Offer to baby-sit so your parents can go to a movie together to relax. You'll be helping your parents a lot by spending time with younger brothers or sisters to reassure them and talk with them about the move. After you move, why not take a younger brother or sister on a tour of the new community, and point out the safe places to walk and play? Remember that your parents really are doing the best they can to make your family's move a success.

In a two-parent family, spouses can share their feelings with each other. But if you live in a single-parent household, your parent may not have anyone to whom he or she can confide fears and worries. A single parent may feel an even greater need to be a "pillar of strength" at this time, so that children won't worry about the move. You can help your single parent by letting him or her know that you don't expect perfection.

FAMILY TALK

At times when your family is together, sometimes it's even worth turning off the TV and taking some time to talk about each person's concerns, hopes, and fears about the move. It will help you all to understand one another's behavior during this difficult time. When your family does get together to have a talk, it's important to remember that each person's view deserves to be heard. Don't tell others their fears aren't important or aren't real. If one person feels something is a problem, it *is* a problem. But try not to leap to the rescue immediately with your solution. Let others express their feelings, even if they get angry! First get the problems out into the open, then you can begin to work out ways to help one another solve them together.

Your family can find more suggestions for family discussions on moving in *Families on the Move* by Patricia Cooney Nida, Ph.D. (Kendall/Hunt Publishing Company, Dubuque, Iowa).

4

It's *Your* Move

Take Control of It!

Moving is a time when you often feel out of control. Your life seems to be something that is happening *to* you, as if guided by some outside force, and you can't do anything about it. Though you can't control everything in your life, there are some things you can control: your thoughts, feelings, and actions. It's true that there may be nothing you can do about the decision to move, or the choice of the house or the new school. But you can control your own personal move by how you think about it, feel about it, and plan for it.

TAKE CONTROL OF FEELINGS

Going through a move, with its ups and downs of emotions, can be bewildering. Sometimes you feel as if you're on a roller coaster gone wild. But once you understand the emotional stages of the change process, you'll know to expect shock, anger, and sadness as normal feelings that come along with the move. You'll also know that these emotions are temporary states that will eventually pass. You can't eliminate the emotions, but you can reduce their negative effect on yourself by understanding why you're feeling them and by venting them in the right direction.

The way you think about something affects the way you feel about it. If you *think* something is threatening you, you will *feel* fear. If you think someone is angry at you, you will feel anger or sadness in return. But if you recognize that the person is not really angry at you but at something else, you will not feel that strong emotional reaction.

You can control your feelings by making sure you're thinking straight. When you find yourself becoming upset, angry, or alarmed at something someone else says or does, stop and examine your thought processes. Train yourself not to jump to conclusions: the first thing that pops into your mind is not necessarily the only explanation. The obvious answer is not always the right one. Stop and ask yourself: what else could be causing this reaction?

There is always more than one way to look at a situation. Human behavior is very complex, and other people's motives for their actions are often not what we think they are. Our own perception is often wrong because we look at things from our own point of view, and because we tend to assume the worst is true.

One night at the dinner table when Chris's parents had a fight, Chris felt awful. They hate each other, he thought, and they hate me too. And it's all my fault because I left the lawnmower out in the rain.

What other logical explanations could Chris have given for his parents' argument? Perhaps they were just tired; or maybe his mother was really sad at having to leave her good job, and the lawnmower was just the last straw.

If you try, you can usually find at least three perfectly good reasons to explain why any crisis occurred. The first reason that comes to mind is likely to be the gloomiest one: let's call it the *gloom-and-doom* explanation. The next one might be a little brighter. It's the *could-be-worse* explanation. And if you really try, you can find another one that's even better. This is the *not-so-bad-after-all* explanation.

Let's say your friend has a fight with you. The gloom-and-doom explanation might be that your friend is a turkey and was never loyal to you in the first place. The could-be-worse explanation might be that your friend is upset because he flunked the spelling quiz—again. And the not-so-bad-after-all explanation: your friend is so sad you're leaving that the only way he can let go is by picking a fight with you and telling you he doesn't really like you anyway.

Whenever there is a crisis, or you find yourself getting upset, angry, or sad, stop and look for at least three logical explanations. Don't stop at the gloom-

and-doom reason. As you search for the other explanations, why not go directly to the source? Ask the person why he said or did this thing. You'll often be surprised to find that the reason is one you hadn't even thought of.

You can also use this technique to explain your own behavior. If you find yourself getting angry or sad, try to think of the real reasons that might be causing those feelings. After you figure it out, you may want to go back and explain to someone why you said something. It will help others avoid misinterpreting your behavior and not take personally something you said or did because you were really reacting to the move.

MINIMIZE CONFUSION

"Go back, wrong way." In simple, direct language this road sign warns misguided travelers of danger ahead. During the change process, when the usual routines and rules are disrupted and people have lots of extra worries, they often become confused and need some plain, clear directions, like that road sign.

Because of the confusion and the sense of isolation you and your family may feel, it's important for family members to keep communicating with one another. When people are under stress, they don't hear as clearly as usual and may not always express themselves as clearly as they think they do. So communication takes longer and must be more direct. You may find that the adults in your family need to give you more directions than usual: what, where, when, how, why. And you may need to ask more questions than usual: what? when? why?

This may cause you some anxiety. You're used to living your life without a lot of this kind of direction, and it may seem they're treating you like a little kid. But again, the real reason is the move. The old rules and routines no longer apply, and the move itself requires a lot of work that must be done by a certain date. Even after you move into your new home, it will take some time until routines are set again. Until then, don't be afraid of asking simple questions, or asking for more directions than usual. And don't be offended when your parents seem more directive. Remind yourself that it's just temporary. Your parents aren't trying to boss you around. They're trying to ensure that all the work gets done on time. Have a talk with your parents about it. Make a bargain with them: until everyone's settled in the new place, you get to pester them with questions, and they get to give you directions, and everyone agrees not to be offended.

GIVE AND TAKE

Bargaining or negotiating is a tool that you can use to cope with the stress of facing a lot of unwanted changes in a short time.

Life had been going along smoothly for Jeanette:

the captain of the football team had invited her to the prom and she had already bought her dress. Then her parents announced they were going to move. Suddenly Jeanette felt as if her life had come crashing down around her; everything was out of her control. The move was planned for the week before the prom: she would have to miss it. And to make matters worse, Jeanette's parents wanted her to come home right after school every day to help her mother and brother paint the house, instead of spending time with her girlfriends. It was bad enough having to leave them, but now it seemed they were being taken from her before she'd even moved.

Jeanette asked her parents if they could make a compromise. She explained how much the prom meant to her, and they agreed she could stay on for it, spend that weekend at her best friend's, and then join her family in their new town. In return, Jeanette agreed to help with the painting cheerfully. As they discussed the problem together, Jeanette's mother suggested Jeanette invite her girlfriends over to help paint. Then they'd all go out for burgers together. In the end, Jeanette got to be with her friends, and her friends felt she still needed them. And the house got painted too! Jeanette felt a lot better about the move because she didn't feel her life was out of control any more.

There may be some things about your move that you can negotiate with your parents. But don't present them with a list of impossible demands, and don't expect to get everything you ask for. You will have to be willing to give up some things too: it has to be give and take. Of course, kids are at a disadvantage in trying to bargain with their parents. In the end, they have to do whatever their parents tell them. But if you're reasonable about it, and if you show a willingness to give as well as take, they should be understanding and willing to allow you some concessions so that the move won't disrupt your life entirely.

CROCODILES & DUCKS

Some problems are big, serious problems. If you're swimming in the river and you see a crocodile coming toward you, even if he's smiling, that's a big, serious problem. Other problems are little problems. If you're swimming in the river and you see a duck coming toward you, that's a little problem. As you go through your move, it's important to distinguish the big problems from the little ones, the crocodiles from the ducks. The crocodiles need immediate attention, and often a cry for help. The ducks don't require that much worry. You can usually push the little critters out of the way by yourself. Because you only have a certain amount of energy in your energy tank, you need to save it for escaping from the crocodiles; you can't afford to waste it on worrying about stray ducks.

If you can't find your green sweater because it's already been packed, that's a "duck." You'll just have to find something else to wear and forget it. You can't afford to let it upset you too much.

If you find yourself becoming more and more depressed and withdrawn after you move and you try to escape through alcohol or drugs, that's a crocodile. Cry help.

If you let the little problems get to you, you can find yourself, as someone said, being "nibbled to death by ducks." But it can only happen if you let it. You may not be able to control the crocodiles in your life without some help, but you should be able to keep the ducks where they belong. You'll find this simple technique will help a lot—whenever you find yourself worrying about something, ask yourself: "Is this really a crocodile or is it just a duck?" Usually the answer is pretty clear! If it's not clear, ask yourself, is this problem still going to matter next week? Next month? Next year? If your reply is no, it's probably a duck. Then, imagine yourself putting the duck back into its pen and locking the door.

TAKE CONTROL OF PLANS

By planning for each phase of the move, as described in the following chapters, you can actually take control of many aspects of your own personal move. The move no longer becomes something that is happening *to* you, but something *you* are doing. When you make the decision to say good-bye to people, places, and things in your old town, you're taking control of the situation. It's *you* who are saying good-bye, because you have chosen to do so. When you do the things suggested in this book to plan ahead for your transition to the new town and school, and get involved right away once you get there, you are making the choice to handle your own move, not let it happen to you.

5

Saying Good-Bye

During the Disconnect Phase, you begin to disconnect yourself from your old place and prepare to move to the new one. You start to say good-bye, not only to friends and acquaintances, but to your surroundings. You begin to relax your grip on your old town and prepare to turn your attention to new places and new experiences. But saying good-bye to the people and places that are important to you can be painful. If it hurts so much, you may wonder, why say good-bye at all?

Before you can turn your attention to the new place, you have to let go of the old. When your hands are full, you can't pick anything up. You literally have to let go of some things so you can pick up others.

But just because you're moving doesn't mean that you're leaving your old life behind completely, or that you have to cut your ties to your old friends. It's true you're moving on, but your old life will always be an important part of you, and even though you may be moving a long distance away, you don't have to lose touch with the people you care about.

The French have two words for good-bye. One of them means "good-bye forever." The other one, which they use much more often, just means "good-bye till we see each other again." When you think about saying good-bye to your friends, don't think of it as "good-bye forever" but just "till we see each other again."

You still have to say good-bye, and this is an important point. Avoiding good-byes may seem easier at the time, but in the long run it leads to an even greater feeling of loss. When Julie knew she would be moving soon to Kenosha, Wisconsin, she couldn't face saying good-bye to her best friend Carmen. Saying good-bye seemed so *final,* almost like making it happen. Perhaps, she thought, if I just don't talk about it, it won't hurt so much. So she never did.

But after Julie moved, she felt she had left something undone. There were so many things she still wanted to tell Carmen. Finally Julie wrote to her. It took fifteen pages, but at the end Julie was sure Carmen would understand how much their friendship had meant, and that it didn't have to end because of the move.

It's better to express your feelings, even if the

partings are emotional. If you don't, you will always feel something is missing—as if you walked out of the theater before the end of the movie. Saying good-bye, even with the pain it brings, is an important part of the moving process, and it actually makes letting go easier.

SAY GOOD-BYE TO PLACES

Besides saying good-bye to the people you care about, you also need to say good-bye to the places that have been part of your life. Many people who get depressed after they move into their new home never got around to saying good-bye to their old one. Jason's family was to move from Saginaw to Bay City, Michigan in August. But Jason had a summer job as a camp counselor which began in June and ran until September. He left his old home for camp but returned in September to the new home, missing out on his family's move altogether. He wasn't there for the block good-bye party, and when his family went to church their last Sunday in town, Jason wasn't with them to hear the minister's farewell. A year after they had moved, Jason found that whenever he dreamed about being at home, his dreams took place in the old house in Saginaw. Although he had not moved a long distance, he still hadn't really disconnected himself from his old home. In his dreams, he was still living there. Jason wished he had taken the time to say his own good-byes.

Before you move, make one last visit to your favorite places—a special beach, perhaps, and the hamburger stand where you and your friends always eat
lunch. Take one last trip around your old town—and
your old house—and just say good-bye to them.

SAY GOOD-BYE TO FRIENDS

Your most important good-byes, of course, will be to
your friends. Go ahead and make a big deal of it. Buy
yourself a fancy address book and collect your
friends' addresses. You'll be thinking of your first-
string friends, but include your second-string friends
too, the ones you just say hello to in the hall, the kids
in the dance band. And don't forget that favorite
teacher, the campus cop who fixed your flat tire in
the parking lot, the vice-principal who was always
there when you needed to talk.

You need to stay in touch with the people who
know and understand you. After you've moved, write
letters to them and send holiday cards. If you have a
cassette tape recorder, you can record your own messages to send, complete with sound effects and music!
You may be able to call special friends occasionally
and even visit, too. Remember, you don't have to let
these friends go forever unless you choose to do so.

Make yourself a scrapbook of your old house and
neighborhood—pressed flowers and leaves from the
garden, snapshots of house, neighbors, friends,

school. When you move, you'll have a permanent record and keepsake to take along.

You may find yourself not wanting to think about something because it reminds you of the move. Go ahead and look forward to the junior prom or the school play, even though you know the next day is moving day. Don't let the move keep you from experiencing the good things that are ahead of you while you're still in your old town.

TAKE MEMORIES ALONG

When you're packing your belongings, don't throw out things you may later wish you had kept. In fact, it's a good idea not to sort through your things when you're angry. Even if you now think you hate school and your friends so much you don't care about your old yearbooks or that pep rally poster you're pitching into the trash, six months from now you may wish you still had some of those mementoes. You can always decide to throw them out next year.

Don't pack all your most precious treasures in the cartons that won't be delivered for weeks. Tuck a few items that mean a lot to you into your suitcase to take along on the trip: a team picture, a snapshot of a friend, or the corsage from the Valentine's Day Dance. That strange motel room or new bedroom will seem more homelike with a few cherished possessions on the dresser.

WHO NEEDS THEM? YOU DO!

As you come out of the initial shock and numbness that occur during the Disconnect Phase, it's common to experience anger. Unfortunately, the anger with which we greet the prospect of making a change in our lives is often directed at the people who mean the most to us. You may feel angry toward your family, or you may find yourself getting short-tempered with your friends. They probably won't understand what you're going through and may demand that you "snap out of it." "Some friends," you tell yourself. "Who needs them? I never liked them anyway." And that makes you even angrier: these are the people you are sad to be leaving, yet you don't even want to speak to them!

If you do find yourself picking a fight with your friends, remind yourself why you're doing it. And be sure you make up with them before you leave.

The friends who are staying behind will be going through some emotional reactions of their own when they learn you are moving. They will also feel shock, anger, and sadness. After all, your move is causing them to experience an unwanted change—they're losing you! They'll feel hurt that you're moving away and leaving them, so without thinking they may lash out at you to hurt back. Although Sandy was unhappy to be leaving her friends, she was excited about moving to Seattle. She thought her friend Diane would be happy for her too. But when she told her, Diane's response was "Ugh, Seattle is a stupid town. I'm glad I'm not going there. I hear the kids are dumb and the teachers are cruel." Sandy was hurt. But Diane didn't really mean it. If your friends say things like that, they don't mean it either. You matter so much to them that losing you is painful, and they can't help hurting back.

It's always easier to pick a fight and get mad than it is to say good-bye; it gives people a good excuse not to have to say those two difficult words, to admit: "You matter a lot to me, and I don't want to lose you."

Just as you may not want to think about the move or face saying good-bye, your friends may also try to escape from the fact that you're leaving. They may be hurting too much to remember to give you a good-bye party. Don't wait for them to do it—give your own good-bye party. And don't be afraid to tell them that you care about them.

6

Old Math?
But I Only Know
New Math

*Preparing to Make Your New Town
Your Hometown*

One of the best ways you can take control of your own personal move is by thinking ahead and planning what you will do after you move. Don't wait till you get there to start making your new town your hometown.

LEARN ABOUT THE PLACE

First, find out about the place you're moving to. Each part of the country has its own unique environment, history, and flavor. If you read up on your new place ahead of time, you'll start to get a feeling for it even before you arrive. Then, after you move, you'll already feel more comfortable about the place because it will be more familiar to you.

If your parents are working with a real estate agent, they're probably receiving information packages about your new town. You should read them too. If you're moving from one military base to another, the family liaison office or family service center at your old installation can give you information about your destination, and once you arrive there, you can get an information package about your new base and locality.

Go to the library and look at maps of the area where your new home will be located. Check out some books about the part of the country you're moving to. Learn about its history, special places, geography, plants, and animals. If you have a special interest, find out about that too. Are you a rockhound? Read up on the geology of your new location. Do you like to cook? What are the traditional dishes of your new area? The more you learn about your new place, the more you will be in control of your environment. And the sooner you learn about it, the sooner you'll feel at home there. Why not start a notebook with the information you find? It will come in handy later.

Learning as much as you can about a place and its people will help you to understand why things are the way they are there. Life in each region of the country is distinctive because it developed out of a unique environment and history.

The kinds of recreation that are common in any particular place also depend on the local climate, geography, and customs. In Colorado they ski, in Florida—well, they don't. But you may learn how to water ski or skin dive. In North Carolina, your school may have a clogging team who are experts at that traditional Appalachian dance.

MAKE UP YOUR OWN MIND

As you find out about your new town, try to avoid being influenced by sweeping generalizations others may make about it. If you hear something terribly bad about a place, or something terribly good, don't rush to form an opinion. People often exaggerate the good and bad things about a place. A travel brochure will only tell you how wonderful things are there. You don't want to be disappointed by expecting something to be better than it really is. At the same time, don't let doomsayers convince you that there's nothing good in your new town. Every place has both good and bad. You want to become aware of both, but keep them in the proper perspective.

Above all, beware of what people who have never lived in your new town say about it. Raul wasn't looking forward to moving from Tampa, Florida, to Galena, Illinois, because his aunt was always talking about how terrible the weather was in the Midwest. Once she'd had a flat tire while driving through during a snowstorm in the winter. But when Raul got there, he found the place was beautiful, not far from the Mississippi River. It did snow a lot during the winter, but during the blizzards school was cancelled! Some of the first ones to criticize a place are people who have never even been there. You really can't get to know a town until you live there yourself.

The good things—and the bad things—in your new town will probably be different from the good things and bad things in your old town, and this may take some getting used to. A person who grew up in New York may feel lost at first in the spacious grandeur of New Mexico. Portland's rain may depress a newcomer from San Diego so much that she doesn't even want to look out the window at the beautiful forest that the rain supports. The natural beauty of Arizona is not the same as that of Vermont, but it has its own uniqueness and loveliness. Try to take your new place on its own terms, instead of judging it by the place where you used to live.

YOUR NEW SCHOOL

The single most important thing you can do to ease your transition to your new school is to make sure that the *transcript,* or copy, of your records from your old school gets transferred to your new school by the time you move. This is not just a formality or useless paperwork. In order to place you in the right classes at the right level, the counselor at your new school needs to know what classes you've already taken. Your transcript is the only thing the counselor has to go on when deciding where to place you.

Many people assume that the old school will automatically forward transcripts to the new school, but it's not true. Your school cannot legally send these confidential records anywhere unless they have written permission from your parents. If parents don't remember to take care of this before the move, the transcript won't be sent.

You can avoid the agony of being placed in the wrong classes by explaining to your parents the need to have your official transcript sent to the school by the time you arrive there. Encourage them to go to your old school and sign the authorization so the school can forward the records promptly.

What if your parents aren't sure where you will be living when you move and won't know which school you'll be attending until you get there? Or what if your transcript is sent to one school, but there's a last-minute change and you end up going to another one? Your new school still won't have your records. By the time your new school gets your parents' authorization to forward to your old school, and your old school sends the transcript, several months may have passed.

Just to make sure your records go where you go, it's a good idea to request an *unofficial transcript* and your *check-out grades* to carry along with you. That way, if there's a last-minute change in schools, you'll still have the vital information you need. Explain to the people at your old school that you're moving and want to be sure you are placed at the right level in your new school. They may release the unofficial transcript to you. If they refuse, get a request from your parents. If they won't give the material to your parents, tell your parents to demand it. The records themselves are the property of the school, but your parents have a legal right to a copy of them. Parents have power in schools, though they don't always use it.

The unofficial transcript is just what it sounds like—unofficial. It contains the same information as the official one, but it is called "unofficial" because it is released to you, not sent directly to the school. Because it might be tampered with, it cannot be used as an official record. Actually, it would be foolish to try to change any information on it: the school would discover the discrepancy when the official transcript arrived. Even if you bring along an unofficial transcript, your new school will still need to have an official one sent from your old school. But the unofficial transcript will give the new school the crucial information needed to place you correctly when you arrive.

The new school needs your official transcript promptly in order to know how many credits you have. If they don't have that information, you may have to repeat work you've already done. Daryl was a high school senior when he moved with his Air Force family to Phoenix, Arizona. He wasn't too happy about having to move during his senior year, but he reasoned that it was only for three more months, then he would graduate. Daryl had already been accepted with a scholarship to Howard University. But though his parents called his old school repeatedly, somehow his official transcript never did arrive at the new school. Without it, he couldn't prove he had enough credits to graduate, and he was told he might have to stay in high school another semester to make up credits he already had. By the time the transcript finally arrived, just before graduation, Daryl and his family were at their wits' end. If your new school doesn't get your official transcript, they can't guarantee you'll graduate on time.

You and your parents have a legal right under federal law to look at any school records that will be forwarded to your new school. (Someone from the school must be present to supervise, in order to ensure that nothing is changed, removed, or added.) If you believe the records may contain material that is negative or might prejudice a new teacher against you, invoke your legal right to see your records. You and your parents also have a right to demand that any negative subjective comments be removed from the records.

VISIT THE SCHOOL

Encourage your parents to look into the schools in the town you're moving to. It may affect their choice of where to choose a house or apartment. Sometimes this involves asking around about the local school districts. If your parents decide on that house on Ash Street, will you be in the West High district, while if they picked the house across the street you would go to East High, a much better school?

When your parents are house-hunting in the new town, suggest that they plan a visit to the school you would be attending if you moved into the neighborhood. Schools usually don't mind such visits. After even a quick tour of a school, your parents will be able to tell whether or not they would want you to go there! But visits must be organized in advance, at the convenience of busy school personnel. Parents should call the head of guidance at the school to arrange a visit.

If you are able to visit your new town before the move, try to arrange a visit to your new school too. Perhaps you can talk to the teachers you will have and even meet some of the kids. Ask teachers if there is any reading you can do so that when you move you will be as close as possible to the others in your class. A pre-move visit will also give you a chance to become familiar with your new school surroundings, and will give you a mental image about what it will be like—

you'll know what the teachers' names are, what the kids look like, and how they dress and talk. Going there and having a look means that it won't be an unknown quantity any more.

Even if you can't go on a trip to your new town before you move, you should still find out as much as you can about your new school. You can find out a lot of information by writing or even making a phone call to the guidance office and talking to a counselor. Explain that you will be a future student at the school. Ask the counselor to send you a copy of the school newspaper so you can become familiar with what is going on there. Also ask for a class description guide and handbook. Explain the activities you've been involved in at your old school and ask the counselor what kinds of activities there are at the new school. Will you have to sign up in advance for a particular program? Are there tryouts that only occur on a certain date? If you want to make a really good impression, write a follow-up letter to the counselor to express thanks and to remind about any material to be sent to you.

If you make your move in the summer, as many families do, don't wait until fall to go to your school for the first time. Most schools want students to pre-register in the summer anyway. School administrative staff are on campus during the summer, and some schools are on year-round schedules so teachers and students may be there too. Be sure your parents go with you when you register. They can talk to the school staff and work out the best program for you, including ways to help you get involved in activities right away.

Don't assume that everything will be exactly the same as at your old school. It may be quite different! When Sharon moved to Maryland and began eighth grade, she felt like she was having to relearn math. She had learned new math at her old school, but her new school taught old math.

High schools' requirements for graduation may differ too, so you'll need to find out how many credits your new school requires, and if there are any additional classes you will have to take. Be sure to get this information as soon as possible, especially if you are a high school junior or senior. You don't want your graduation to be delayed because you didn't find out in time that you needed another science class.

THE SILVER LINING

They say that every cloud has a silver lining. Every move has a positive side too, no matter how much the rest of it hurts. Your move may be your chance for new experiences, travel, adventure, new friends. And there may be some things—or some people—you'll be glad to get away from. Perhaps there are some things about yourself you'd like to leave behind too. The move will give you an opportunity to do that.

It's hard to change a reputation once it has been established, but when you move, you can leave it behind altogether and begin in the new school with a clean slate. If you aren't happy with the social group you've been going around with, or if you got off to a bad start in French and feel the teacher has always treated you as a dumbbell in that class, or if you had a bad experience that you'd rather forget, you'll be able to leave all that behind when you move. No one in the new school will know you by that old childhood nickname you could never get rid of; no one in the new school will know you got in trouble for throwing eggs at the principal's car on Halloween. This move may be your chance to make a fresh start.

7

You're Off!

Going from Here to There

At last the day comes when everything is packed into boxes and ready to go. And it's time for you to go, too. You are now in the Change Phase.

While the physical move itself may take place without any emotion, there's likely to be one last crisis as you're leaving: in all the confusion, the dog gets out into the street, or someone's finger is slammed in the door on the way out. Craig's family was getting into the car to drive to their new home in Mobile, Alabama, when his four-year-old sister Stacy discovered that "Blankey" was missing. Their mother had decided this would be a good time to separate her from the filthy scrap of blanket she always carried around, and she had thrown it away. In tears, Stacy refused to budge until she got her security blanket back, and the whole family joined the fight.

Your move may take place in any of several ways. The parent who has been transferred may have had to go on ahead of everyone else and live in a hotel in order to start work. Or your parents may leave you with relatives while they do the heavy moving themselves. Or you may all go together—by car, train, bus, or plane.

If part of the family goes on ahead, they may not appreciate the difficulties those left behind have to face. Gil's father had to go on ahead to his new job in Buffalo, New York, so Gil, his mother, and two sisters had to do all the packing and moving themselves. As soon as they walked out the door, his little sister started screaming and the cat ran away. They drove cross-country in their Honda Civic, and their Irish setter was carsick during the whole trip. When they finally got to Buffalo, they found their father living in a nice hotel, eating in fancy restaurants, and peeved at them for being such grouches.

Your family may decide that the trip gives them a good chance to visit relatives along the way. After all, since you're moving, you may not see them again for a long time. But in fact, it may not turn out just the way everyone expects. Dave's father was looking forward to visiting his parents in St. Louis, Missouri, on their way to Eliot, Maine. He couldn't talk of anything but Grandma's homemade gingersnaps and how much fun it would be to go fishing with his Cousin Hershie. But when they got there, Cousin Hershie was in the hospital having a hernia operation, and

Grandma had no intention of baking cookies—her office was getting ready for the budget review! Your relatives can't stop their lives just because you're coming into town. They're going to be busy with their usual activities, and you are going to be under some strain from your trip. So don't be disappointed if the ideal visit proves less than ideal. You and Dad go fishing yourselves, or bake some chocolate chip cookies to surprise Grandma when she comes home from work.

The adults in your family may decide to ship you off to relatives while they do the work of moving themselves. If so, don't take it as an insult. It's not that you don't count, or that they don't care what you think about it, or that they don't want you to be part of their experience. Moving is hard work and boring. It's true that it will be easier on them if they don't have to keep track of the care, feeding, and entertainment of kids while making sure the mover doesn't put the box of weight-lifting equipment on top of the hundred-year-old porcelain teapot. But they also are trying to spare you some of that hard work and boredom. So don't let yourself start thinking they don't care. Instead, try to enjoy yourself where you are. But don't sit around waiting for someone else to entertain you. You're probably going to have to take responsibility for your own entertainment.

WHEN YOU ALL GO TOGETHER

If your family goes together by bus, train, or car, you will all have to be around each other for a long time. But it will also give you some time to adjust to the transition from the old place to the new one. If you go directly by air, your move will take less time, but you will also have less time to make the transition.

If you drive across the country, you can plan to make it more than just a boring ride. Offer to plan the trip before you go. Get a detailed highway map and examine your route. If you will pass by a special attraction, you might want to ask your parents whether you could work it into the trip if you have time. Don't expect to hit every tourist attraction from here to there, but it can help break the monotony of the trip if you can do even a little sightseeing. You might not have time to spend a full day at Disney World, but it would be a shame to drive within a few miles of the Grand Canyon and not take a peek. Get the family together to discuss the places you would all like to see.

Pack up a special box of things for the trip— games; maps of your route; snacks; books; writing paper, envelopes, and stamps for writing to friends; camera and film for taking pictures. Don't forget to include in your suitcase some things that will make the motel room more familiar, such as a favorite picture or object.

While you're riding in the car on a long trip, you can only count so many out-of-state license plates and cows before you're ready to scream. To break the boredom, bring along a book of games for travelers. Word games that everyone in the family can play together are good because they keep people talking and avoid the sense of isolation that tends to develop.

Include some plans for physical activity when you take a break. Although some drivers want to keep going and cover "just another hundred miles," all experts agree that frequent stops are better for travelers in the long run, by helping to keep the driver alert. It's important to give your body a chance to move around after sitting in a cramped position for hours. So when you do take a break at a rest stop, don't sit in the car! Get out and get some exercise.

When passing through a town, for a change from restaurants your family might like to stop at a grocery store for simple sandwich makings or visit a delicatessen and then take your picnic to the local park.

If you're traveling with an animal, bring a cage or carrier and don't forget a leash. Even if Fluffy always loved to ride in the car before, don't expect her to make it all the way to Wichita sitting on people's laps. Fluffy may have loved to ride along on a quick trip to the store, but she is sure to lose her patience on the great trek west. Two days out of Albany, you may think you have a tiger not in your tank but in your lap.

Don't leave animals alone in the car while you're

sightseeing, especially in an unfamiliar climate. It may get dangerously hot or cold for them.

Why not make an expedition out of the trip itself? Keep a diary and take pictures. If you collect samples of plant life, remember that some states are strict about keeping out anything that may carry pests. Don't try to smuggle fruit or other live plant material across state lines. Just because you can't see any bugs doesn't mean that the microscopic eggs are not inside the fruit. You don't want to give hitchhiking fruit flies a lift into your new state!

As the millionth telephone pole flashes by and there's nothing but static on the radio because you're too many miles from nowhere to tune in a station, you may find yourself anxious to get to your new town. Will you make the baseball team? Will you like your new bedroom? Will you meet someone wonderful and fall in love? There are some things you just can't do anything about until you get there, so don't let them distract you from your trip. Enjoy it as much as you can. You may never get to do it again.

8

But There's Nothing to Do in New York!

Moving In

When you move into your new home, you begin the Reconnect Phase. But as you begin to plug yourself into your new place, it's normal to feel somewhat disoriented and let down.

After months of preparation and worrying about the move, when Dana moved to Stamford, Connecticut, she breathed a sigh of relief. It's all over now, she thought, and I can get back to living a normal life again. But after a few weeks she found things still didn't feel normal. Kids talked to her in class, but every day at lunch she sat by herself in a corner—all the other seats were "saved." It was supposed to get better after we moved, she thought. And that made her feel even sadder.

In fact, it is often *after* a move that people experience the highest anger and lowest depression. Some have called this period "the gray days."

Why? You aren't used to your new home. You don't have a mental map of your new town yet, and it's frustrating not to know your way around. You haven't gotten used to the new school or made friends yet. And you still miss the people you left behind.

After you've moved in, there will be brief periods of ups and downs, and then one day things will seem normal again. It's really over at last, you'll want to think. But not yet. You're beginning to get back to normal, true, but be prepared for a few more bumps on the road before everything's smooth again. It can take from six to eighteen months to get completely settled into a new place and feel at home again.

YOU'LL STILL BE YOU

Many people anticipate a move with unrealistic expectations. They expect that the move will change them somehow, or that problems they had before the move will magically disappear. If you approach the move with unrealistic expectations, reality can be a strong shock. After Brad got used to the idea of moving from Gainesville, Georgia, to Anaheim, California, he started to think about what it might be like after the move. Disneyland was in Anaheim—he could go to Disneyland every weekend! And it wasn't far from the ocean—he'd get a surfboard and be a surfer. He could already see himself lying on the beach beside his board, tanning in the sun, his hair bleaching to a pale California gold. In his fantasy, the girls on the beach had eyes only for him.

But six months after Brad moved, he was more depressed than ever. He had only been to Disneyland once with his family; it had poured rain and his little brother had screamed all day in his stroller. Going to the beach was not what he expected, either—the first time he went, he got sunburned so badly it hurt all over; the second time, he tried surfing but couldn't even paddle the board out past the breaking waves. When a fish bumped into his leg, it scared him out of his wits. He hadn't really thought about the fact that there were fish—maybe even sharks—swimming below him in the ocean. And on the beach the girls didn't even know he was there. In his fantasies about moving to California, Brad had imagined the move would turn him into a different person. But after he moved he was the same old Brad.

After you move, you're going to be the same person you were before you moved. Moving to New York won't make you a Broadway star; moving to Florida won't make you tall, slim, and blond, if you're short, fat, and brunette. Moving to California won't make you a better tennis player—unless you take lessons, of course.

GETTING ORIENTED IN
YOUR NEW HOMETOWN

First, take steps to make yourself feel at home in your new home. As soon as you move in, try to make your new room comfortable and familiar. Put up your favorite posters, that funny picture you took at the swim party last summer, your trophies, the things that make you happy when you look at them.

Have a family talk about which parts of the new house are for what purposes. You may need to make some trade-offs. The attic room, where your mother has her paints and easel, might be off limits to everyone else, while the basement playroom is a free zone —okay to play in and mess up within reason.

Then start to get oriented to your new town by getting to know your new neighborhood. Walk around and become familiar with your surroundings. Get a map of your new town (try the Chamber of Commerce) and mark your house on it. Now get someone to help you mark out the routes to school and other important locations. You'll probably need to keep the map with you for a while until you know your way around.

Suggest that the family go on an exploring trip around the town just to see where things are in your new community: supermarket, department store, theater, library, schools, parks, etc. Include the places each person in the family is interested in.

Put a map of the town on a bulletin board at home where everyone in the family can pin up little notes on it to mark the locations of things they've found—a bowling alley, a bicycle repair shop, or an ice cream parlor that has great sodas. Every city has its dangers—mark those too: an unsafe part of town, a busy street with no sidewalks, a drainage channel where small children shouldn't play, a house where a large Doberman always jumps the fence when people walk by.

Encourage your family to do some fun things right away in your new town. Remember, you may have to look a little harder to find those fun things at first. If you're from the East Coast and you're moving to the West Coast, you may think there are no recreational activities if there's no ice skating or sledding in the winter. If you've always lived on a ranch outside Big Timber, Montana, you may think there's nothing to do in New York!

GETTING SETTLED IN THE NEW SCHOOL

If your family has chosen to move during the school year, don't be upset. You may find it's actually easier for you than moving in the summer. Moving in the middle of the school year means you'll have more opportunities to make friends. If you move in the summer, you still won't know anyone when you arrive, and you may not have much chance to meet new friends until school starts.

If you arrive at your new school in the middle of the year, the teacher will know you are a new student, but if you are beginning at the start of a school year, the teacher will probably *not* know you are new to the school unless you go up and tell her. Teachers often don't know which kids were there the year before, so it's important to let your teachers know you're a newcomer.

You might expect that all the schools in the country would teach the same things, but they don't. This means that, even if you have prepared well for your transition to your new school, you'll probably be out of step with the rest of the class in some subjects. You may be ahead of everyone else in math, while you may be behind them in Spanish.

You may find you've never even had some of the subjects taught in your new school. Some schools are traditional, others are experimental. The times at which different subjects are introduced vary, too. Every state and locality includes its own local history and culture as a subject. If you grew up in the Northwest, you will know all about potlatches, but when you move to North Carolina, they'll think you're dumb if you don't know how to use a gee-haw whimmydiddle.

ASK FOR HELP

If you find you're out of step in a particular class, don't be afraid to ask your teacher for help. Teachers won't know you need help unless you say so. Don't be afraid to explain to your teachers that you haven't had a certain subject. Teachers are there to see that you learn what they have to teach, and most will be glad to give you the help you need to catch up. Counselors are also there to help, and don't be too shy to ask them about anything. That's their job, after all.

Don't expect to pick up material you don't understand by just sitting there. One of the authors of this book still recalls how embarrassed she was on her first day as a second-grader at the American School in Berchtesgaden, Germany, when she was asked to go up to the blackboard and divide a word into syllables. She had never heard of a syllable before, but was too ashamed to tell the teacher so. Of course she didn't divide the word correctly, and the teacher thought she was a pretty stupid kid! Eventually she figured it out herself, but had that been algebra or geometry she wouldn't have been so lucky.

Your new school's standards may differ from those of your old school. What was A work in one school may be B work in another. If you find you're very far behind the rest of your class, talk to your teacher or ask your parents to do so. It can be embarrassing to go down a level, but it may be the best solution for you in the long run. It doesn't have to be forever. You may be able to move back into the other class after you catch up. Don't stay in a class that's too difficult—you'll be miserable! Perhaps some extra tutoring is all you need to get into step.

If you're ahead of the rest of the class, ask to go

forward a level. Even if you think it will be easy to sit through the same material again, you'll find it's also terribly boring.

If you aren't out of step with the rest of the class, but you still find your work slipping at first, don't become alarmed. The confusion and disorientation of beginning in a new place can distract your attention and affect your work. Don't expect yourself to be running at one hundred percent power when you first arrive. But if you still have problems after a couple of weeks, talk to your parents, teacher, or counselor about getting some extra help.

Be sure the school nurse knows of any special health problems you have which might require immediate attention in case of a crisis, such as a severe allergy, epilepsy, a heart condition, or sickle cell anemia. The school nurse, like other school staff members, is there to help you and can be a supportive person you can always turn to for help and as a friend.

MAKING FRIENDS

The most frustrating part of starting out in a new town and school is that you don't know anyone, and no one in the new place knows *you*. You haven't suddenly lost your talents or your achievements, but no one in the new school knows how good a shortstop or costume designer or piccolo player you are. You'll have to prove yourself all over again—your skills and abilities, the fact that you're a worthwhile person to have as a friend.

Don't expect to have a full set of new friends two weeks after you move in. Making friends takes time. Don't feel you have to accept the friendship of whoever latches onto you first, or you may be disappointed later. This is another aspect of your life that you can control: you can control who you choose as your friends.

Every school has its own groups or cliques of kids who are friends. Some of these cliques are clearly defined by dress, hairstyle, makeup, and behavior. It may seem that they're as rigid as the Indian caste system, and impossible to break into. But in your new school there are certain to be a lot of kids who don't fit into any of those categories—and don't want to either.

The kids at the new school will take your clothes, hairstyle, makeup, and behavior as clues to where they think you fit in, but these clues may have a different meaning from the ones they had in your old town. If you don't want to be placed in the wrong category, avoid extreme clothing styles that make a loud "statement." It's best to stay "neutral" for a while until you find your niche in the new place.

DON'T BE VULNERABLE

If you belonged to a tightly knit group of friends in your old town, it can be depressing to find yourself suddenly an outsider. Keep reminding yourself that this is only a temporary condition. If you remember that, you won't be vulnerable to people who may try to make friends with you for the wrong reasons.

When Marc moved to Colorado, he was depressed because after two weeks at school he still hadn't made any friends. When Rodney came up to him and invited him to join him after school, he was delighted. At last, here was a friend! But after school, when the two went off together, Rodney had a little business to take care of first. Marc was dismayed when he saw what the business was. It turned out that the person who had "befriended" Marc was the biggest drug dealer in the school.

Marc didn't know what to do. After all, Rodney had been the only person in school to offer him friendship. Feeling helpless, Marc hung around with Rodney, hoping he could make some better friends later. But the rest of the kids at the school put him into the same category as Rodney, and the ones he wanted to meet kept their distance.

If Marc hadn't felt so desperate for friends, he might not have gotten himself into such a situation. Often people like Rodney seek out newcomers like Marc because they sense that they are vulnerable. They know that the new kid won't be aware of their bad reputation. Don't feel you have to take up with the first person or the first group that claims you, especially if they don't seem to be the kind of kids you would want to have for your friends at your old school.

On the other hand, some people may latch onto you and tell you to avoid certain boys or girls. It may be good advice, or it may just be jealous gossip. You wouldn't want others to judge you before they got to know you, so give them the same chance, and make up your *own* mind.

But don't wait for friends to come to you. You can and should get out and make friends yourself.

THEY'RE SHY TOO

"I can't do that!" you may say. "I'm too shy." But if you really want to make friends, you'll probably have to make the first move. You may find it hard to believe, but other people are just as shy as you are. They may want to get to know you better, but they just don't have enough courage to approach you! Surprising though it seems, they may be afraid *you* will reject them.

All of us share that deep fear of rejection, and because of it, we will often avoid approaching people we would like to know. Usually we're not aware of it; we make up other excuses for not going up to people we want to meet: "She looks like she has enough friends already." "He wouldn't want to be my friend." "I just don't feel like talking to him today." If you find yourself making those kinds of excuses, ask yourself: "Why am I really avoiding it? Am I just afraid that he or she will say no?"

Think about that for a minute. What if he or she

did say no? Could you take it? Is the risk of having someone say no worth the chance of making a good friend? Of course it is. You can take a no! And if you do get a no, refuse to let yourself take it personally. This is a good time to remember to think straight: maybe there's another reason for that no. Maybe that boy can't show you around town after school because he has soccer practice. Or perhaps he has to go for math tutoring but is embarrassed to admit it, so he just gave you a vague excuse. Whatever the reason, remind yourself that the no has nothing to do with you or your worth as a person. And if someone really snubs you, you can be sure that the person is just a turkey anyway, and not someone you would want for a friend after all!

TAKE THE FIRST STEP

How do you start a conversation with someone you would like to get to know? You might begin by asking the person something; then he or she will have to answer, at least. Ask him something about himself: most people would rather talk about themselves than anything else, anyway. It's always flattering when someone else shows they're interested in what you think, and it should lead to positive feelings right away.

Compliment her clothing, his book report, the goal she made in the soccer game. Or ask for the other person's opinion on something. You could also try asking for help or advice. How do you get to the library? What kinds of questions does Mrs. Petrocelli usually ask on her English tests?

Smile and look at the person when you talk, even if you're so embarrassed that you just want to mumble and look at the ground. No one wants a friend who always mumbles and looks at the ground! Don't try to do all the talking yourself. The other person will feel that it has been a satisfying conversation if he or she does the talking. You'll have time later; your goal right now is to start to make friends, not to tell your life story to anyone who will listen.

Shyness is hard to overcome, but you *can* do it; you can take control of it and decide you're going to be brave, even at the risk of getting a no. If you can do that, you'll find that it will help you greatly in taking control of your feelings, and, in fact, your whole life now and in the future.

GET INVOLVED

The very best way to make friends in a new town is to get involved in activities right away. Every school has after-school clubs and sports. Find out what they are, and join one that interests you. You probably don't even have to know how to ski to join the ski club, or how to dance to join the dance club. Were you on the swim team at your old school? Talk to the coach about trying out. Were you in scouts? Find out about the scouting organization in your new town.

Ask someone what activities are going on at lunchtime in the library or resource room. There may be a chess tournament or some other game or club meeting that interests you. Not only will this give you the opportunity to meet other kids, but it will give you something to do during lunchtime, the loneliest time of the day for a newcomer. At club meetings and in games and sports, you're sure to meet others who share an interest, some of whom may end up becoming your close friends.

Or you may meet other kids through them. When Lauri moved to Salt Lake City, Utah, she didn't know anyone at all. She had been involved in the hiking club at her old school and joined the one in her new school. There, she met Sue, who introduced her to her sister Joanne. Lauri and Sue never became very close, but three months later Lauri and Joanne were best friends.

Get involved in the activities you participated in at your old school even if you're not really interested in them anymore. Join the orchestra even if you're tired of playing the flute! Think of it as a way to get to know people. But don't try to outdo everybody else. You won't make friends by showing them how much better you are. After you've been there a while, you can display your talents.

Why not volunteer to help out at school? Offer to be a teacher's aide, an office aide, or to work in the library, cafeteria, or with the custodian. Helping out will give you lots of opportunities to talk to people and get to know them.

You'll probably find it easier to make friends in your elective classes—home economics, shop, band, art—than in required classes such as English or math. The atmosphere is usually less competitive and there's more opportunity for students to talk with one another as they work on projects.

How about getting involved in student government? It doesn't mean you have to run for student body president. Attend a meeting of the student body organization. Volunteer to help out on a committee —decorating for a dance, perhaps, or planning an event.

Your religious group will also have a youth organization you can join. There you'll be bound to meet other kids with whom you will have something in common. If you live on a military base, be sure to get involved in activities at the youth activities center too.

You might like to consider beginning a new sport or activity where everyone else is a beginner too. Archery lessons at the park? A gourmet cooking class?

You may feel that you must be the only new kid in school, but there probably are others too. Ask your teachers who else is new. You may be surprised to find that there are more than you think. It may be easier to make friends with other new kids—they won't have any friends either! You might even start a club. You'll all have something in common!

If your school has a welcoming group or big brother/big sister program for newcomers, you're lucky. If not, after you become settled into your new school, why not suggest it to the Student Council, or to the teacher who is their advisor? You'll probably find that the student officers are very concerned about encouraging new, as well as old, "invisible" students to become involved in activities. Getting involved in such a project may prove very satisfying to you—you'll be able to sympathize and understand the problems of other new students. Some "Tips for Forming a Welcomers Club" are included at the back of this book.

When you do start to make friends, there are some key things that you should remember. The kids you meet will not want to hear all about the place you came from. You may have loved it in Williamsburg, Virginia, or Coeur d'Alene, Idaho, or Auckland, New Zealand. But when you tell your new friends about it, don't be surprised if they get bored or annoyed and change the subject. They may be jealous and think you're just showing off. Basically they really don't care because it didn't happen to *them*.

Don't tell your new friends what's wrong with their town and why your old town was better. You'll only sound conceited. We all think our own hometown is best. You may feel that the climate in Phoenix is terrible compared to Knoxville, but to someone who has lived in Phoenix all his or her life, it is the not only the best but the only climate in the world! It's natural for you to feel loyalty to your old town (and it may indeed have been better!), but now your new town is your hometown, and you'll have to start becoming loyal to it. Search for the things that make your new town special, and concentrate on its good qualities instead of its bad ones.

It may seem like a hopeless task to make "lots of friends." But remember, all you really need is *one* friend. Once you make that one friend, he or she will open the door to others as the person introduces you to his or her own group of friends.

As you begin settling into your new home, town, and school, don't forget to keep up the communication among family members. Suggest a family meeting to discuss the problems each one is having adjusting to your new place, and don't forget to share the good things you've found about the new town.

Keep in contact with your old friends, too. Write to them or get permission to make a special call once in a while if it's long distance. Perhaps you can invite a friend to visit you during vacation. You may even be able to introduce your old friend to some new friends in your new hometown.

9

To Board or Not to Board

Is it for You?

Your first reaction to the news of a move may be "Not me! I'm not going anywhere!" And you may feel you want to look around for friends or relatives to stay with instead of moving with your family. Boarding with friends or relatives is an option that should be considered with care. Sometimes it is the best solution, sometimes not—it all depends on your individual situation. To board or not to board is a decision you and your parents should make only after examining all sides of the question.

For any teenager, an upcoming family move can be a terribly difficult prospect. If you are a high school senior about to be graduated and heading for college, that move can be devastating. In such a case, remaining behind in your old town and boarding with another family may be the right decision. But what if you're not a senior, but a junior who has just made the varsity football team after struggling hard to achieve this goal? That's not so clear cut. If you were good enough to make the team in your old town, you're probably good enough to make the team in your new town. In your case, some kind of a compromise might prove a better solution.

LIST YOUR OPTIONS

If you're considering the option of boarding, first make a list of all the alternatives available to you, and all the good things and bad things that could result from each possible choice. For example, one option might be to stay behind only until the end of a semester and then join your family.

Think about it carefully: what if you do stay behind after the rest of your family moves? You may be angry at them now, but after they're gone, you'll miss them. That separation will be hard on you. It might even prove more painful than it would have been to go along with your family in the first place.

Don't expect boarding to give you more freedom than you had at home. If you board with friends or relatives, you'll be under the control of the adults of the household. Because you are not their own child, they will feel responsible for your welfare and are likely to be even stricter with you than your own parents! They don't know you as well as your parents do

—they don't know how much trust or independence you've had in your own home. They only know that it's their responsibility—legally and personally—if anything happens to you. Your best friend's father may have seemed like an easygoing, permissive parent, but after you move in he may turn into a iron-fisted jailer. Your own parents might have yelled at you when you stayed out until midnight on weekends, but your friend's parents may be reluctant to let you go out at all.

WHAT ARE YOUR REASONS?

Ask yourself honestly why you really want to stay behind when your family moves. Do you have a good reason? Are you close to graduation? Are you in a special program that isn't offered at the new school? Are you going to miss out on a goal you have worked hard to achieve?

Or is your reason something else? Are you trying to assert yourself against your parents? Are you punishing them for making you move? Are you trying to avoid the move itself? Or are you expecting to have more freedom in another home? If so, boarding is almost certainly *not* the right answer for you. You'll probably find that it creates more problems than it solves.

If you are considering boarding because you can't face the anguish of moving away from your friends, or because you are afraid you won't make new ones, boarding probably is not the right decision for you either. It's hard, and you may not want to let yourself believe it, but you *will* make friends in your new town. And don't forget—just because you're moving away doesn't mean you have to give up the friends in your old town.

SET THE GROUND RULES

If you do decide to board, everyone concerned—you, your parents, and the adults with whom you will be staying—should agree on some basic ground rules. You and your parents should come to an understanding on these issues first, then both sets of parents should agree on them.

Finances. Your parents will be paying for room and board, but what about your spending money? Will you have access to emergency money in case something comes up? What about the ski club weekend trip to the mountains? Telephone privileges? Clothing money? Expenses for team uniforms?

Household Chores. You should know in advance what chores will be expected of you. Don't expect to move in as the princess who doesn't lift a finger, but you don't want to end up as Cinderella who has to do the dishes every night.

Freedom. What time will you be expected to be home at night on week nights? Weekends? What about overnight and weekend trips? Dating? Driving privileges?

Study. How many hours a night will you be expected to study? What grade standards will you be expected to meet?

Medical Emergencies. Be sure the family you'll be staying with has any necessary medical information including your doctor's name and phone number, information about allergies and any medical problems you may have. Both sets of parents should agree ahead of time what to do if a medical emergency should arise.

Religious Attendance. Will you be expected to attend religious services with the family you're staying with?

Once the ground rules are set, it would be a good idea to put them down in writing, so that there will be no misunderstandings later. You don't want to find out after your parents are in Ankara, Turkey, that the adults you're staying with expect you home at nine o'clock on weekends, though your parents always let you stay out till midnight!

10

The Rain in Spain
Is Mainly a Pain

Moving Overseas

If you are moving overseas, you are in for an experience that will be one of the most rewarding and most challenging of your entire life. You will get a chance to meet people, to go places, and to do things that most people never get to do. You will gain a perspective of your host country, of the world, and of yourself that will enrich your life. A foreign move also presents special difficulties and puts more emotional —and sometimes physical—strain on you than a move within your own country. But if you know what to expect, if you prepare well, and if you approach your overseas move with an open mind and a sense

106

of humor, in the end you will probably feel that it was all worth it—many times over.

When you move from one part of the United States to another, many things are new and unfamiliar, and you don't know your way around at first. But when you move to a different country, not only will you not know your way around, but you may not even know how to read the street signs or how to ask directions to get where you want to go. The sights, the sounds, and the smells will be different. The food, the houses, and the people will be different. The everyday chores of daily survival will be difficult and confusing at first. And the long hours of travel required in an overseas move will be especially exhausting to you and your family.

Whenever we make a change, we face the unknown, and that makes us somewhat fearful. In a foreign country, where so much is unfamiliar, that fear can be greater, especially if you can't even talk to people at first. This just means you'll have to do some extra planning and preparation so that when you move overseas, the unknown won't be so unknown, the unfamiliar will become familiar, and you'll soon be able to talk to people, understand what is going on around you, make friends, and get the most out of your overseas stay.

As soon as the shock wears off, you will greet the prospect of an overseas move with excitement. Visions of castles and ski lodges and palm trees will dance in your head. But when you arrive at your destination, you'll find that there are indeed castles, but there are also rude waiters; there are ski lodges, but there are also leaky roofs; there are palm trees, but you may have to view them through your mosquito net.

If you aren't prepared to accept some difficult things in the bargain, the disappointment—and even betrayal—you may feel can ruin your overseas experience. If you do acknowledge that it will be difficult at times, those difficulties won't be so hard to face. Also remember that you can decide to overcome those difficulties and that they will become fewer as time passes and you learn your way around the new country and culture.

LEARN ABOUT YOUR NEW COUNTRY

The best way you can prepare for a foreign move is to find out all you can about the place you're going to. Learn about the country, its land and resources. Learn about the people, their history and famous figures, their religion and culture.

Go to the library and check out some books about the place you're going. The more you read up on it, the more prepared you'll be. Even though you'll be a resident, not a tourist, tourist guidebooks are very useful for practical and up-to-date information on the monetary system, transportation, weather, and such details as what kind of electrical current the country has. (Will you need an adapter for your hairdryer?) But you'll need more in-depth information than the brief overview given in a tourist guidebook. Will you need a permit to bring in items such as a tape recorder, camera, or stereo? Is there a quarantine period for pets? The country's consulate or embassy can answer such questions. Your family may have to get some information from government agencies at home. For example, your parents may not be aware that an export permit from the United States Department of Commerce is required to take an American-made computer into a foreign country.

Read up on what's going on today in the country. Look in the *Reader's Guide to Periodical Literature* at your library for recent articles about events in the country. It's important to know about the country's history, but it also helps to know what happened last week.

See if your library has a copy of the "Country Study" (previously called "Area Handbook") for the country you're going to. These books, prepared for United States Government agencies, are also available at United States Government Printing Office bookstores and by mail from the Superintendent of Documents, United States Government Printing Office, Washington, DC 20402.

A book you will find extremely useful in learning to understand other peoples and adjust to life overseas is *Survival Kit for Overseas Living* by L. Robert Kohls (available from Intercultural Press, 70 West Hubbard Street, Chicago, IL 60610).

TALK TO SOMEONE

Perhaps the best source of information about any particular country is a person from that country. Arrange to talk to someone before you go. You can find out if there is a foreign exchange student from the country living in your area by asking the exchange student at your high school—he or she will have a list of all the other foreign students in the area. If you find that there is one from the place you're going, call the person up and invite him or her over to tell you about life there. Most people are delighted to be able to provide information about life "back home."

A foreign exchange student may even be able to give you the names and addresses of family or friends. Don't be shy about getting in touch with them when you arrive there. It may be your passport to new friendships overseas!

When you talk to someone from the country, you'll want to know much more than where the major tourists sights are. You'll want to know the things that *aren't* in the tourist guides.

Dress. What kind of clothing is considered appropriate for girls and boys to wear in public? When entertaining friends at home? In some countries, you could be arrested for wearing shorts on the street. Even in less strict countries, your clothing is often taken as a signal of your morality. Scanty, tight, or "hippie" clothing or hairstyles may be taken as an advertisement that the girl wearing them is "available"—to anyone. This kind of misunderstanding is a reason American girls have a bad reputation in some countries.

Shopping. How do people shop, and where? Is bargaining expected? Or are you expected to bargain only in the bazaar or open market, but not in a shop that has price tags on the merchandise? How do you shop? In some countries it is considered rude to pick up merchandise yourself—you're supposed to ask the shopkeeper for it, even if it is right in front of you!

School. What will school be like? How are students expected to behave toward teachers? Is asking questions in class considered bright or rude? What's the proper dress for school?

Dating. What are the typical forms of recreation for teens? What are the dating customs? In many countries, teenagers don't go out on dates as couples. They always go out together in groups. Asking a girl to go out alone may be practically a proposal of marriage!

Gestures. Most people worry about learning the language when they go to a country. But you also need to learn the "body language" and gestures that people use to communicate almost as much as they use speech. How do people greet others? Do they bow, shake hands, kiss cheeks? Is there a difference when greeting members of the opposite sex? What gestures are considered impolite? In some countries, sitting with crossed legs is seen as very rude. What are the proper and improper table manners?

How do you gesture "yes," "no," "come here," and "good-bye"? In many countries, these common gestures are almost opposite to the ones we use: the gesture for "come here" may be the same one Americans use for "good-bye." That can cause some confusion!

And what gestures are insulting or vulgar? You should know what they are, not so you can use them when you get mad at someone, but so you'll be sure you don't use them by mistake. The American gestures "thumbs up" and "A-OK" are actually vulgar insults in several countries.

LEARN THE LANGUAGE

One of the most important things you can do to prepare yourself for a foreign move is to learn the language of the country. Start right away; the more you can learn before you go, the easier it will be for you when you arrive. Don't expect people in other countries to speak English. Contrary to what many Americans believe, English is not the international language.

You'll want to learn the language of your new country so you can get around by yourself, make yourself understood, and understand others, but there is another, even more important reason you should make learning the language your top priority. If you learn the language of the country you are going to, the people you meet there will respect you, welcome you, and offer you their friendship. If you expect to get by on English, you will find that the only people you ever meet are other Americans and people whose business is dealing with American tourists. If you don't learn the language, you'll never get beneath the surface of the rich culture around you.

FIND AN INTEREST

When John's father, a computer technician, was transferred to Frankfurt, Germany, John had mixed feelings about the move. He was a junior in high school and didn't know what he wanted to do after graduation. He'd never been much interested in foreign languages or history, but he liked music and played the piano fairly well. He decided that as long as he was moving to Europe, he might as well keep up with his music. He went to concerts and took lessons from a retired music professor. Through his piano teacher John met other young music students, was invited to their homes, met their families, and gained an insight into life there that he never would have had if he had just hung around other Americans. During vacation, when John's family wanted to go home for a visit, John wanted to stay on for a special music festival. He had become so excited about it that he decided that he wanted to go to college and study music.

Find a special interest that you can explore in depth once you get to the country. Are you interested in sports? Every country has its own, though they may be somewhat different from the ones you're used to. Are you a musician or dancer? Make it your project to learn all about the traditional music or dance of the country. You might even decide to learn how to play the koto or the bouzoukee. As you explore your special interest, you'll find that the inner life of the country and people will open up to you. You'll discover and experience first-hand the many different threads that are intertwined in the tapestry of culture. Having a special interest to explore is also likely to lead to friendships you might never have made otherwise.

LEARN THE CULTURE

The other most valuable preparation you can make for your overseas move is to learn about the culture of the country you're going to. Culture means more than art galleries, opera, and ballet. Culture means all the ways of thinking, feeling, perceiving, believing, and acting that are shared by a group of people. Culture holds the clue to people's attitudes, behavior, and all of the aspects of life in that country which, as a foreigner, you will find bewildering and confusing.

At the heart of every culture are certain basic assumptions about the nature of man and his place in the universe, his relationship to his physical environment, to other people, and to the forces of the unknown. From these basic concepts come all the various aspects of culture: how people live their daily lives, how they do their work, how they deal with other people, how they worship, and how they play.

Because these basic concepts may be quite different in different cultures, they give rise to different attitudes toward any given situation. For example, American culture values individualism and personal privacy, while other cultures place more importance upon the group. If you go in your room and lock the door, another American will think that you don't want to be disturbed, while someone from another culture may think you are being aloof and secretive. When the phone doesn't work, a person whose cultural view holds that man has no control over his physical environment may shrug it off as a fact of life, while an American, believing that man must dominate his environment, will rush to get the repairman! But if the repairman belongs to the first culture, there will be conflict.

When people of one culture try to deal with people from another culture, conflict and misunderstanding often result. It is as if two people were trying to play a game together—but each one is playing by a different set of rules. Each person thinks the other is cheating!

You are used to playing by the rules of American

life. The rules of life in Saudi Arabia or Mexico or France are different—not wrong, not better or worse, just different from the ones you're used to. You need to learn the rules of life in the place where you're going to be living.

This doesn't mean you will throw out all your own rules. It doesn't mean you will give up being who you are or will adopt the new culture. But while you are in the country, you must live within its culture, so you must go along with its basic rules. This is a courtesy a guest must give to any host, in this case, a host country. After all, you would expect a visitor to the United States to follow the basic rules of American life. Just because people come from London or Tokyo, where they drive on the left side of the road, doesn't mean they can do that here! Remember, while you are overseas, you are the guest; you are the foreigner in someone else's homeland.

SEEING YOURSELF THROUGH OTHER EYES

Once you understand something of the culture, you'll begin to understand why the people around you act as they do. You'll learn to see them on their own terms. You'll also see how they regard others from their own point of view. Your experiences in developing cultural perspective may give you some unexpected insights.

Sherry's mother, a medical anthropologist, brought Sherry along on a summer field trip to Yucatan, Mexico. In the village, the first time Sherry had to go to the toilet, she asked an old woman where it was. The woman pointed out behind the house to the compound where the horses and cows and pigs were. When Sherry explained to the woman how Americans had toilets in their houses, the old woman showed surprise and disgust. "You mean you always go in the same place?" she said. "How unsanitary!"

One of the things you'll have to deal with is the peculiar image that people in other countries have of Americans. But when you realize that, in most cases, their only contact with Americans has been through tourists, television, movies, and what they read in the newspaper, it's not hard to understand how they could get such a distorted picture.

You may meet people who think all Americans are rich, or that if you come from Chicago you must be a gangster, or if you're a Texan you must have an oil well in your backyard, or if you're an American girl you'll go to bed on the first date. If you tell them they're wrong, they may protest: "But I must be right —I saw it in the movies!" It's frustrating to be judged by an inaccurate stereotype, but when people get to know you, they'll learn what you're really like. Just as you wouldn't want to have others judge you by a stereotype, try not to do the same yourself. Keep an open mind and make your judgments after you have found out for yourself.

GETTING USED TO IT

The sense of losing control of your life, which is normal in any move, becomes greater when you move overseas. There are more things to lose control of: you don't know the language, you don't know the customs, and you don't know if that stinky bean curd you're being offered is supposed to be eaten or used as an insect repellent. You can gain control of your life by solving those problems—that is, by learning the language and the customs. And by keeping your sense of humor when you learn you are supposed to eat the stinky bean curd after all.

When you move overseas, you go through the same stages as you do in any move. When you first arrive, you will be in a state of shock. The reality that you are actually in a different country may take a while to sink in. It seems incredible to believe that just yesterday you were in Kansas City eating a hamburger and today you are in Barcelona eating paella.

You've probably built up a lot of excitement about the trip and have been looking forward to it. No matter how well you prepare yourself, you'll probably find that the place you imagined is quite different from the real one. As your initial excitement starts to wear off, you may find yourself getting angry at the discrepancies between the imagined place and the real place. "This is not the way it is supposed to be!" you may say.

Even if you know you should expect cultural differences, you're likely to react instinctively against ways that are different from your own. When Carolyn arrived in Rome, the first thing she wanted to do was order a pizza. When it came, it wasn't anything like the pizza back home. "What's the matter with these people?" she said angrily. "Didn't anyone ever teach them how to make pizza the right way?"

Your first few weeks abroad will be a challenge as you learn to deal with the daily chores of life. A simple task like going to school on the metro or getting a meal in a restaurant can be a bewildering ordeal at first. But remind yourself that it won't always be so frustrating. The second time you go on the metro, it will be easier. The tenth time, it will be a snap. The twentieth time, you'll be giving a tourist directions like a native.

The first thing you have to do is reestablish your "mental map." Once you do, you'll feel confident you "own" your territory, even if that territory is Cochabamba or Kuala Lumpur. For your own and your family's peace of mind and to prevent confusion, be sure you always carry emergency information—know how to reach your parents at work, as well as the local police, fire department, a reliable doctor, and the American consulate. You will probably never need to use that information, but you will always know you are prepared just in case.

As with any move, it takes a long period of time to become adjusted. A foreign move usually takes even longer, because there are so many more things to get used to. The demands of dealing with a foreign culture and language, and the constant decisions you have to make, will be very draining emotionally, so you need to be sure that your "energy tank" doesn't run out of gas. Give yourself plenty of time to get settled, and don't make a lot of demands on yourself as soon as you arrive. You don't have to see every castle in Germany the first weekend.

Go ahead and stick to familiar foods and places at first. Would your family really be more comfortable going to the hotel restaurant where you know they speak English instead of that floating noodle shop on a sampan you heard about? You can always try the noodle shop after you feel a little more at ease. But don't forget to get out and try the local foods, see the sights, and visit the castles. Seek out new places and experiences gradually as you feel ready for them.

A new town in any country—even your own—is bewildering at first. Start as you would in any other new community. First get to know your own neighborhood. Walk around and explore. Meet your neighbors. Suggest the family go exploring together on weekends. Where are the local shops? The bus stop or the subway station? Ask someone who knows the area to show you around. When are shops open? Do they close in the afternoon for a few hours, or on a certain day of the week? How do you use the money? The public transportation? What does that sign mean? What are the main landmarks and any dangers you should be aware of?

In some countries you will have to learn to be

more careful in public than you had to be at home. The reality of terrorism has made this an unfortunate necessity. Never touch an abandoned package or suitcase—it might contain a bomb. And don't walk away from your own baggage—you might be mistaken for a terrorist! In some countries you must be prepared to be searched by the bomb squad when you enter a public place. Understand that they're only concerned for your safety and everyone else's—they're not singling you out for harrassment.

Whenever your family moves, there's a certain amount of confusion, and your parents will need to give more directions than usual until everyone gets settled and learns the ropes. In a foreign country they may need to give even more direction. Your parents may tend to be more protective of you overseas, too. Even if they trusted you to run around freely at home, they may be reluctant to let you go out by yourself at all when you first arrive. Try to understand it from their point of view. They're still not sure what's safe and what isn't. After a while, when you both feel more sure of yourselves in the new place, they won't feel so much anxiety and will be confident you can get around safely on your own.

BRACE FOR CULTURE SHOCK

Even if you go abroad well prepared for your adventure, you are likely to experience some degree of "culture shock." Culture shock is the term that has been given to describe the typical emotional reactions people feel as they adjust to living in a different culture. The symptoms are much the same as the ones that come with any move: anger, frustration, depression, a wish to go back to the way things were before the change, a feeling that "these people here just don't do things right," a sense of being out of control.

You can't avoid a certain amount of culture shock, but you can lessen its effect by understanding what you're going through. It's a normal reaction, and it will pass. At this difficult time, be sure to keep communication open with your family and the friends you make. Don't listen to Americans who hate it there; look for an American who likes it there and can explain the puzzling things to you.

You'll find you must learn to do without some of the things you're used to. Go ahead and let yourself get angry at first, but after you've let off steam try to find something to fill its place. If there's only one television station and it only shows historical soap operas in a language you don't know, find out what else people do for entertainment. And do it. They may not have McDonald's, but what do they have instead? Every culture has its own fast food goodies—felafel, tacos, piroshki, steamed pork buns. Look for the things that make your place special and unique. You'll find much to appreciate if you look for those things and decide you're going to enjoy them.

Without rejecting your own values, try not to let your own cultural prejudices keep you from trying new things. Go ahead and try the snails—think of them as *escargots*, not as the icky creatures that left slime all over the pansies at home. Trying new things doesn't mean, however, that you should ignore your common sense or break your own cultural rules. There are some things that you wouldn't do at home that you shouldn't do abroad either. If you object to snails because they're not kosher, you have a perfect right to say no, wherever you are! You may run into some situations where local kids tell you, "Everyone does it," but they're really bending or breaking the rules of their own culture. Ask yourself: would *their* parents approve if they knew?

Keep your sense of humor. Learn to laugh at yourself too, if you make a cultural slip. And remind yourself that this is a temporary situation. You *are* going to learn your way around; you *are* going to become comfortable and competent in your new environment.

When people do something that angers or puzzles you, remember to think straight. Find out *why* they did it. Try to think of things from the point of view of the other culture. If your new friend said he'd go snorkeling with you but stood you up because his aunt came over, your first reaction may be that he did it because he's rude or doesn't really like you or want you for a friend. But perhaps it really is because in his culture the family relationship is so strong that all plans with friends are automatically cancelled when a relative unexpectedly arrives.

Since you are moving overseas with your family, in a way you are lucky. You'll be bringing along your own little island of home—people who know you, people you can talk to about your needs and fears. But existing family tensions can be strained further by the pressure of being in an unfamiliar place and being forced to spend more time together before you all know your way around and have made friends. That means you'll have to be especially sure to keep communication open and take care of each other.

Until you speak the language, you'll need to communicate in English. Try to meet someone from the country who speaks English—don't rely on other Americans exclusively. You'll want to have some American friends too, but it's easy to meet other Americans—they tend to find each other without much trouble. If you only hang around with other Americans, however, you will never make friends with local kids. A good way to meet kids from the country is through the youth group of your religion. Also ask your parents if the people they work with have any teenagers—you may be able to make some good friends that way.

Get out and do things. Don't isolate yourself or stay at home—and that includes just hanging around the post, the base, or the American ghetto.

Acknowledge your feelings of loneliness and longing for the friends who are far away. Write letters, or send cassette messages to them. Do whatever you have to do to get those feelings out so they don't stay trapped inside.

It's not easy to live in a foreign country. The feelings of depression and sadness you may feel can become so overwhelming that they make you want to escape. But above all, don't be foolish enough to get involved with drugs in a foreign country. Drugs will not help you get over those feelings, and they may well cause you more problems than you ever dreamed of. Most foreign countries have much harsher drug and alcohol laws than those in the United States, including long prison terms and even execution! As long as you are a guest in the country, you are subject to its laws, and unlike the United States, in some countries people are presumed *guilty* until proven *innocent.* The American consulate cannot get you out of jail if you break the country's laws. The last thing you want to do is learn about the country from the inside of one of its prisons.

While you're living abroad, remember that you are a guest in the country, and that the way you act will form the basis for the impression people there have about America and Americans. If you prepare well for your overseas move, keep your sense of humor, get ready to ride out the ups and downs of culture shock, and make a genuine effort to learn about the people and the culture and to appreciate them on their own terms, you will find that your time overseas is one of the most exciting and memorable adventures of your life.

11

Going Home Again

Returning from Overseas

Your overseas adventure is over. It's time to go home again. You can hardly wait to get back to your friends, to your old town, and to a Big Mac. If only you can get your feet on American soil, you think, everything will be all right. But whether you are going back to the states after a year in Kyoto, or even if you are returning to Boston after having lived in Dallas, you may find that going home is not as easy as you expected. Returning to the United States after an overseas move can be even more difficult than going abroad in the first place.

HOME HAS CHANGED

Although we know that time doesn't stand still, and that things change, somehow we expect that *home* will never change—that when we return, everything will be as it was when we left. It can be a shock to find that nearly everything has changed—the country, your town, your friends, and even yourself.

If you come back to the town you lived in before you went abroad, you may hardly recognize it as the one you left behind. Your favorite burger stand may now be a parking lot. The empty lot where your mother once made you let all your pet mice go may be a block of condominiums. Your old house may now be the onramp for the eastbound tollway.

Even if you don't return to a previous hometown, you'll probably feel that the country isn't the way you remember it. We tend to remember things as better than they really are, and to recall that at home people are always friendly, the streets are clean, and the telephones work. When the telephones don't work we feel angry and cheated. Because it's so unexpected, it can be more of a culture shock than some experiences abroad.

Your friends will also seem changed. Some may not even be there any more—they may have moved away. Your best friend may have become best friends with someone else. Your friends may be glad to have you back, but you may not feel that you really belong there as you once did. When you go overseas, you expect to be out of place as a foreigner, but when you come home, you expect to fit right in again. When you don't, it can be very painful. If I don't belong at home, you may think, where in the world do I belong?

YOU HAVE CHANGED

During the time you were overseas, you have changed too. Your values and your outlook on life have been shaped by your experience there, while your friends' values have been shaped by what was going on while you were gone. You have lived through an entirely different set of experiences than they have. In a way you're like Rip Van Winkle, who woke up after sleeping for twenty years. You weren't there for the teachers' strike or the tornado everyone's talking about. The songs on the radio are unfamiliar. You're out of step with the latest fad. You don't know the current slang.

You may feel a gap between yourself and your friends that goes even deeper. Your old friends may seem childish and immature to you. Because of your experience abroad, you've probably developed wider interests, more independence, a more mature outlook, and a different perspective. As you look at life and the people back home, you may be disappointed in what you see.

Just as you experienced anger and frustration at the people when you went overseas, you may find yourself feeling the same reactions toward the people at home. "Why can't those turkeys see that I'm the same person I was before?" you ask yourself. After you finally became comfortable doing things in the other country, you may find yourself feeling anger at the way they're done back home. You may also find yourself feeling angry at your parents—just when you got used to living abroad, made friends, fell in love, they dragged you home again! And home has proved to be a disappointment.

Or you may find yourself feeling angry at yourself: someone else would have been able to fit right in, you think. Maybe there's something wrong with me.

There's nothing wrong with you. The anger, frustration, and sense of being let down are a normal part of the experience of going home after an overseas move. And going home is much harder than people expect.

ACCEPT THEM TOO

In a way, going home is like going overseas. You're coming from another culture (you've *finally* gotten used to it!) and you're thrust into a way of doing things that is unfamiliar. You've come to see the United States through the eyes of another culture, and your attitudes, beliefs, and views may have changed. Just as you had to learn to accept the people on their own terms overseas, you'll have to do the same thing for the people at home. It may seem to you that their views are limited and even prejudiced; but you can't change them. You have to accept them as they are.

When you come home, you may find you miss

things you never thought you would. Sheila couldn't wait to get home to the States after two years in England. She was dying for a real hamburger and a chocolate malt. But five days and five hamburgers later, she realized she was sick of them. What she wouldn't give for a cornish pasty, a rock bun, or a scone with jam and clotted cream. You may even find yourself missing things you thought you hated over there. What you wouldn't give for some of that wonderful stinky bean curd!

DECISIONS, DECISIONS

Some of the things you once took for granted at home will now seem bewildering. You've been away from the wide range of choices that America's abundance of goods presents to us every day. Suddenly you're confronted again with a smorgasbord of alternatives—and, therefore, decisions to make. There's no other country in the world where you must choose between having skiers, flowers, teddy bears, mountains, eagles, monograms, clouds, or covered wagons printed on bank checks; and did you ever really count how many kinds of doughnuts Winchell's makes? When you come home exhausted from the trip, suffering from jet lag, and weary of the long-term strain of having to survive in a foreign culture, your energy tank is already running low. At a time like that, you may feel you just can't take being asked to make a lot of little trivial decisions.

Once again, you need to get back some control in your life. Take time to rest up, and don't make a lot of demands on yourself until you start to get used to things.

Get in touch with others who can offer support. Talk with your family—they will be sharing the same experience of disorientation on returning home. Talking together with them will assure you that you're not the only one having a hard time adjusting to home. Others who have lived overseas will be sympathetic, since they've probably gone through the same thing.

Once you get home, your family responsibilities are likely to change, and that may take some getting used to. You may have had a housekeeper or a maid while you lived abroad, but after you come home, you're going to have to get used to doing the dishes again! If your family did have servants overseas, your parents will need some extra help and support too— they'll have even more household duties to adjust to.

FRIENDS CAN'T UNDERSTAND

Your friends may find it hard to believe that anyone could have difficulty getting used to home, and they may not be as sympathetic as you expect. It's one of those things that you have to experience in order to understand. Although they will be glad to see you, they won't really be able to appreciate your experiences and adventures.

After Scott's family came home from a posting to the American consulate in Moscow, Scott's old friend Don was glad to see him and wanted to know all about it. Scott started to tell him, but after a few minutes Don changed the subject—to talk about some little thing he had done in English class. Scott was hurt and confused. He hadn't even begun to tell Don about the adventures he'd had being followed by the KGB, getting lost on the Moscow subway, and about the girl he met on the plane to Paris on the way home. Don wasn't even interested!

It isn't because they don't care about you, or because they think that your experiences weren't exciting or worthwhile. They aren't really interested because those adventures didn't happen to them. Don't try to force them to listen to your stories, or they'll only get angry at you and accuse you of bragging. They're likely to be jealous, too. Why should you deserve all those adventures? You'll just have to save your travelog until you can find people with whom you can share your memories.

But don't let other people's negative reactions make you feel negative about your experience overseas. Don't try to block it out or to forget that it happened. Be proud of it, enjoy your memories, your keepsakes, and the knowledge, experience, and friendships you gained. They're precious, and they're yours forever. Don't forget to keep in touch with the friends you made overseas. By now they will be an important part of your life.

As soon as you get home, get involved again.

Make your own life happen. Don't come home and withdraw into your memories. Acknowledge that things won't go smoothly at first, but remind yourself there's nothing wrong with you or your family. Then become part of the community again. Join a club, get started in an activity. Eventually you'll find you're fitting in again, getting back into the swing of things—home at last.

Appendix

Tips for Forming a Welcomers Club at Your School

* Make it a club with interesting activities so people will want to join and will get to know each other in a relaxed, enjoyable environment.

* New kids need most:
    (1) a starting point to begin making new friends
    (2) information about the school

* Provide a "welcomer" for each new "newcomer." It's not enough to take the new kids around school once and show them where the cafeteria and lockers are. Welcomers should take them

134

to lunch and introduce them to their own friends. Lunchtime is often the loneliest part of the day for newcomers. Make sure they aren't alone at lunch.

* Plan frequent social activities for new kids and anyone else who would like to participate: a party, a barbecue, a softball game, bowling, etc. But if you plan a party, make sure you include some games that require people to *mix* and talk to people they don't know, otherwise no one will get acquainted. Start off with an ice-breaking activity so kids will have to talk to one another. For example, write the names of different animals on pieces of paper. Think of some hard ones: emu, tapir, three-toed sloth. Tape one to each person's back as they arrive, but don't let them see it! They have to discover what animal they are by asking questions of others at the party, but they can only ask questions that can be answered yes or no.

* Get in touch with newcomers as soon as possible. Make sure your Welcomers Club keeps in touch with the guidance office so you can find out the names of new kids as soon as possible.

* Perhaps you can even get in touch with newcomers before they arrive. Write and send information about your school, town, area, etc. Think: what would you want to know if you were new in your town? You could send a copy of your

school paper, a class description guide, a sample bulletin, information about what it's like there—how people dress, what kinds of activities there are. Ask the newcomers what special information they would like: Dance? Sports? The Honors English program? It's very important that the information newcomers are given is accurate. Don't say you're sure of something if you're not.

* Welcomers should stay in contact with their newcomers for at least a month. Welcomers and newcomers assigned to each other may not be compatible. But they don't have to be friends forever. The point is to get the newcomers to start making their own friends. Each person will eventually find the friends that fit that individual's personality.

Good luck!